The Official
NBC Viewer's Guide

1988
OLYMPIC
GAMES
SEOUL

PINDAR PRESS

PUBLISHER/Harvey Rubin

CREATIVE DIRECTOR/Joan Walton • **EDITOR**/Michael Rosenthal

ASSOCIATE EDITOR/Stephen Malley
ASSISTANT EDITORS/Joe Guise and Cathy Sylvis

ASSOCIATE PUBLISHERS/Charles Powell and Sheldon Rubin
ADMINISTRATIVE DIRECTOR/Sonja Léobold
ADMINISTRATIVE ASSISTANT/Alice Federico

ART ASSISTANT/Laura Bonapace
RESEARCH ASSISTANT/Jodie Fink

Photo Credits

Cover: Focus on Sports (FOS). **3:** Paul J. Sutton/Duomo. **4-5:** Steven E. Sutton/Duomo. **6-7:** 1, 2, 4: The Bettmann Archive; 3: New York Public Library (NYPL); 5: UPI/Bettmann Newsphotos. **8-9:** 1, 3: NYPL; 2, 4, 5, 6: UPI/Bettmann Newsphotos. **10-11:** 1, 2, 3, 5, 6: UPI/Bettmann Newsphotos; 4: NYPL. **12:** 1: UPI/Bettmann Newsphotos; 2: The Bettmann Archive/BBC Hulton; 3: NYPL. **14:** Bob Martin/Allsport. **14-15:** Gray Mortimore/Allsport. **16:** Jean-Marc Barey/Allsport/Vandystadt. **17:** David Madison/Duomo. **18:** Gray Mortimore/Allsport. **19:** Walter Iooss Jr. © 1984 Fuji Photo Film, U.S.A., Inc. **20, 21:** Bob Martin/Allsport. **22:** Allsport/ Vandystadt. **23:** David Madison/Duomo. **24-25:** Tony Duffy/Allsport. **26:** Bob Martin/Allsport. **27:** Steve Powell/Allsport. **28:** Tony Duffy/Allsport. **28-29:** Duomo. **29:** Michael King/Allsport. **30-32:** Tony Duffy/Allsport. **33:** Paul J. Sutton/Duomo. **34-36:** Mike Powell/ Allsport. **37:** Tony Duffy/Allsport. **38-39:** Trevor Jones/Allsport. **40:** Bob Martin/Allsport. **41:** © Dave Black, 1988. **42:** Steven E. Sutton/Duomo. **43:** © Dave Black, 1988. **44:** David Madison/Duomo. **45:** © Dave Black, 1988. **46:** FOS. **47:** © Dave Black, 1988. **48-49:** Courtesy of Wolfgang Schreiber/International Shooting Union. **50-53:** Tony Duffy/Allsport. **54:** Michael King/Allsport. **55:** Budd Symes/Allsport. **56-57:** FOS. **58-59:** Allsport/Vandystadt. **60-61:** Allsport. **61:** Dan Helms/Duomo. **62-63:** David Cannon/Allsport. **64:** Steven E. Sutton/Duomo. **65:** Tony Duffy/Allsport. **66-67:** FOS. **68:** Dan Helms/Duomo. **69:** Mike Powell/Allsport. **70:** Allsport. **71-72:** Tony Duffy/Allsport. **73:** © Dave Black, 1988. **74:** David Cannon/Allsport. **74-75:** Michael King/Allsport. **76-77:** Dan Helms/Duomo. **78-81:** Allsport/Vandystadt. **82-83:** Steve Powell/ Allsport. **84:** FOS. **85:** Paul J. Sutton/Duomo. **86:** FOS. **87:** David Madison/Duomo. **88:** Tony Duffy/Allsport. **89:** Adam J. Stoltman/Duomo. **91:** John Gichigi/Allsport. **92-94:** FOS. **95:** Mike Powell/Allsport. **96:** FOS. **97:** David Madison/Duomo. **98:** Allsport. **99:** FOS. **100-101:** Bob Martin/Allsport. **102-103:** Steve Powell/Allsport. **103:** Mike Powell/Allsport. **104:** C. Cole/ Allsport. **105:** John Gichigi/Allsport.

Acknowledgments

Pindar Press gratefully acknowledges the help and cooperation of the following individuals and organizations in the preparation of this publication: National Broadcasting Company, Inc.: Peter Diamond: vice president, programs, Olympics; Sam Flood and Jeff Zucker, Olympic researchers; Donna Morris, research coordinator; Stacey Malin, research assistant. The United States Olympic Committee; National Archery Association; The Athletics Congress of the USA; Amateur Basketball Association of the USA; USA Amateur Boxing Federation; American Canoe Association; U.S. Cycling Federation; U.S. Diving; American Horse Shows Association; U.S. Fencing Association; Field Hockey Association of America; U.S. Field Hockey Association; U.S. Gymnastics Federation; U.S. Judo; U.S. Modern Pentathlon Association; U.S. Rowing Association of America; National Rifle Association of America; U.S. Soccer Federation; U.S. Swimming; U.S. Synchronized Swimming; U.S. Table Tennis Association; U.S. Team Handball Federation; U.S. Tennis Association; U.S. Volleyball Association; U.S. Water Polo; U.S. Weightlifting Federation; USA Wrestling; U.S. Yacht Racing Union.

Lithography by Case-Hoyt Corp.
Paper by Champion International
Typography by Boro Typographers, Inc.

Library of Congress
Catalog Card Number: 88-61739
ISBN 0-918223-88-1

Factual information, such as world records, and writer's observations regarding athletes, competing countries, etc., are all as of June 1, 1988.

On the cover: Great Britain's Sebastian Coe on his way to the gold medal in the 1500 at the 1984 Games.

Right: Hodori, the 1988 official Olympic mascot.

Contents *(arranged by year of entry)*

INTRODUCTION

In 1896 at Athens, 295 athletes from thirteen nations participated in forty-four events to inaugurate the modern Olympics. In 1988, more than 11,000 athletes from 161 countries will gather in Seoul to compete in 237 events at the XXIV Olympiad.

The enormous growth of the Olympic Games attests to the simple truth which their founder, Baron Pierre de Coubertin, grasped almost a century ago: that gifted athletes from different parts of the globe would welcome the chance to come together and compete against each other for the honor of winning. The fascination such competition holds for us is made clear by the more than one billion people the world over who will follow the Games on television.

Not since Tokyo in 1964 have the Games been held in Asia. In preparation for them, South Korea—the "Land of the Morning Calm"—has been extraordinarily busy, constructing the most spectacular facilities in Olympic history. Two new sites were built especially for the Games—the Seoul Sports Complex completed in 1984 and the Olympic Park completed in 1988. Most of the major events will take place in these two venues, which are only three miles apart.

NBC has devoted unparalleled resources to bring you every feature of the human drama unfolding at Seoul. An Olympic production staff of 1,100, including 500 technicians utilizing a broadcast center built by the Koreans especially for the Games, 45 million dollars worth of equipment and an expert team of sports and news anchors will provide 179.5 hours of coverage, more than 75 percent of it live. An extraordinarily sophisticated satellite network means that the intimate close-ups you will see of athletes' successes and failures will have traveled approximately 89,600 miles before finally arriving on your television screen.

And to help you enjoy the Games — to appreciate their history, understand the separate events, and recognize outstanding performers — we have designed this Official Viewer's Guide. Here you will find vital information about each sport and, at the back of the Guide, details of scheduling and television coverage, in addition to an extensive section of Olympic records. To give you an idea of how the Games have developed, the sports appear in the Guide in the order in which they were introduced into the Olympics, together with their year of entry.

We hope the Guide will contribute to making the truly international spectacle of September 16-October 2 a memorable personal experience for each of you.

—Michael Rosenthal, Editor

The Olympic Stadium, Seoul.

THE SUMMER GAMES

by E.J. Kahn Jr.

1

2

When the Summer Games of the XXIV Olympiad get underway at Seoul on September 16th (September 17th in Korea), there will be competitions in twenty-three sports, of which two will be new ones: tennis and table tennis. (Well, not entirely new, but renovated; lawn tennis was in the Games for twenty-eight years, up to 1924, and the roster of gold medalists accordingly bears such celebrated names as Helen Wills and Hazel Wightman.) Since the modern Olympics were launched at Athens in 1896, the Games have embraced many competitions that to contemporary sports fans might seem bizarre: mountain-climbing, club-swinging, court tennis, croquet, underwater swimming, and tug-of-war. The Paris Olympics of 1900 featured fishing contests in the Seine. Fly-casting came later.

The earliest Games put on in the United States, at St. Louis in 1904, included special occasions called Anthropological Days, in the course of which, among other things, purported African tribesmen engaged in mock Olympic events. At Stockholm in 1912, entrants in the shot put, discus and javelin were judged on performances with both arms. Subsequent Games have also harbored demonstration sports — baseball at Tokyo in 1964, tennis at Mexico City in 1968, taekwondo slated for Seoul this fall. Billiards and skydiving have been proposed along the way but to date not endorsed, as opposed to such now official carryings-on as rhythmic gymnastics and synchronized swimming, which made their debut at Los Angeles in 1984 — twelve years after the descent from the Olympic throne of the legendary Avery Brundage, who, however people may have felt about his political views or authoritarian manners, must surely

....

E.J. Kahn Jr., author of twenty-five books and staff writer at *The New Yorker*, has been the magazine's Olympic correspondent since 1964. His most recent book, *Year of Change: More about the New Yorker and Me*, will be published in the fall.

be credited with doing more than any modern man to make the Olympics the extraordinary spectacle they are today.

I have been a faithful and appreciative attendant at the Summer Olympics only since 1964, so I never got to see a diversion that gave spectators in Greece, circa 520 B.C., much amusement — foot races among soldiers clad in heavy armor. I am less sorry that I missed a chance to witness perhaps the most renowned of classical Greek events. That was the pankration, which dates back to 648 B.C. — a one-on-one confrontation combining boxing, wrestling, kicking, biting, choking, eye-gouging and bone-breaking, and the participants in which were as coddled and pampered as any present-day athletes. The pankration's popularity derived in part from an occasional fatality, but one could avoid this by, if

DATE	HOST CITY	NATIONS	ATHLETES	EVENTS
1896	Athens	13	295	42
1900	Paris	22	1077	60
1904	St. Louis	12	554	67
1908	London	23	2034	104
1912	Stockholm	28	2054	106
1916	Berlin	Cancelled, World War I		
1920	Antwerp	29	2591	154
1924	Paris	44	3075	137
1928	Amsterdam	46	2971	120
1932	Los Angeles	37	1408	124
1936	Berlin	49	3980	142
1940	Tokyo	Cancelled, World War II		
1944	London	Cancelled, World War II		
1948	London	59	4062	138
1952	Helsinki	69	5867	149
1956	Melbourne	67	3500	148
1960	Rome	83	5396	150
1964	Tokyo	93	5586	162
1968	Mexico City	112	6626	172
1972	Munich	122	8144	196
1976	Montreal	88	6189	199
1980	Moscow	81	5923	203
1984	Los Angeles	141	7078	220
1988	Seoul	161*	11,000+*	237

*Latest available estimate

one's shoulders weren't fractured, raising an arm to concede. Spartans, whose code of behavior did not countenance surrender, tended to skip the pankration. (A non-Spartan trainer of one pankratiast who was being strangled once exclaimed, "What a beautiful funeral not to give up at Olympia.") The Twentieth Century, as far as I know, has yet to produce an Olympic athlete who, like the pankratiast Polydamas of Scotussa, killed a lion with his bare hands.

The Ancient Games, memorialized in Pindaric odes and so consequential that Aristotle once dropped everything else to revise lists of bygone champions, date back to 776 B.C. when Coroebus won a foot race of about two hundred meters. The early Games went on for five days, and to enable competitors from warring states to get to Olympia unharmed a truce was observed — first for a month and then, as men set off from more remote places, three months. (Some six centuries would pass in that relatively enlightened era before anyone charged anyone else with using drugs — the accusation coming after a man from Gaul allegedly took an undeserved first in a sprint because all his rivals had succumbed to a magic potion.) The old-time Games went on for more than a thousand years, but they began to deteriorate toward the end of that stretch, after Greece had fallen prey to Rome. It was indicative of their sorry state around 60 A.D. that when the emperor Nero was thrown to the ground during an Olympic chariot race, the event was halted until a substitute driver could take over; in the end the pyromaniacal fiddler was declared the winner anyway.

1] Engraving by A. Castaigne of the pankration in the ancient Olympic Games, in which contestants mauled and occasionally even killed each other.

2] The inventor of the modern Olympic Games, Baron Pierre de Coubertin of France, born in 1863.

3] Helen Wills of the U.S., who won an Olympic gold medal in tennis in 1924 before it was banished from the Games. Tennis returns this year at Seoul.

4] Sixth-century Greek vase painting celebrating the long-distance runner.

5] One of the early Olympic events which is not likely to return — the tug of war, here between Belgium and Holland in 1920.

1

2

3

Nero might have appreciated two latter-day men—both far abler athletes than he was—who for the better part of seventy-six years ran the Olympics, hordes of gifted contestants notwithstanding, pretty much as one-man shows. (And what dazzling world-riveting shows haven't they become!) The first of this remarkable pair was a Parisian boulevardier born in 1863, Baron Pierre de Coubertin. While still in his twenties, he resolved to revive the Olympics. Others, in Greece and elsewhere, had toyed with the notion, but de Coubertin had the means and the determination to do something about it. He began, in 1889, by establishing a Union des Sociétés Francaises de Sports Athletiques. In June 1894, it sponsored a Paris conference on amateurism—one of de Coubertin's life-long loves—that attracted seventy-nine delegates from twelve countries. That

spawned the International Olympic Committee, and he became its first president.

De Coubertin thought about the Olympics, which was most of the time, he was given—as would be Brundage in his turn—to high-flown prose: "The Olympic movement tends to bring together in a radiant union all the qualities which guide mankind to perfection." The Baron played football (the American soccer) and tennis, rode horseback, bicycled and took boxing and fencing lessons. (Longtime Swiss resident though he was, he had little use for any winter sports.) Rowing was his favorite pastime, and at 72 he was a familiar sight pulling oars on Lake Geneva. He died in September 1937 in Lausanne, where he'd moved when he planted the Olympic flag there in 1915.

De Coubertin's first Olympics were held

in April 1896 at, fittingly, Athens. Athletes from thirteen countries took part in forty-four events. Americans won nine of twelve track and field events. (The best performance in the high jump was just short of six feet.) The marathon was an understandably major event, and it was won, again fittingly, by a Greek—a shepherd whose name is usually transliterated as Spiridon Louis. Greece earned nine other gold medals that inaugural year and over the ensuing decade, but only one Greek, featherweight Stylianos Mygiakis, has triumphed in Greco-Roman wrestling. Still, there are many nations in the Olympic family—Bhutan, Qatar, Tonga, and so on—that have never come close to winning any sort of medal, and some of which would not even be on the scene were not their delegations' expenses underwritten by the I.O.C. and the host city. De Coubertin was not against

that; he was all in favor of universal representation, and indeed the parades of far-flung athletes during the opening and closing ceremonies have become highlights of the Games. In the Baron's view, the word that best described the Olympic spirit was not "victorious" but "joyful." There is a monument dedicated to him at the ruins of Olympia, to which many of us aficionados of the Games have dutifully made pilgrimage; and de Coubertin's heart, at his request, is buried there.

Avery Brundage, who was on hand for that ceremonial interment, was of humbler origins, but by the time he took over the I.O.C. in 1952, he had made millions in the construction business. He was an outstanding athlete and a member of the American squad—pentathlon and decathlon—chosen for the Stockholm Games, where it was his misfortune to have to compete against, among other stalwarts, his teammate Jim Thorpe, whose medals were later taken away (though posthumously restored) because he had played some professional baseball. Lieutenant George S. Patton Jr., subsequently a pistol-packing general, might well have won a gold in the modern pentathlon in 1912 except that one of his twenty pistol shots was judged to have missed the target altogether. Patton argued vainly that actually he had scored a double—two bullets through the same precise hole.

De Coubertin and Brundage, who died in 1975, were both emphatically opposed to excess nationalism, which so often became a problem for the Games. As too many Americans yet seem to be unaware, too much flagwaving can backfire. There was so much flourishing of the home-country colors at Tokyo in 1964 that a Japanese rider's horse got rattled and balked at a crucial jump.

It has not always been thus. Back in 1896, there was no official United States team. Most of the athletes were students dispatched to Athens by a Boston athletic club. The very first winner of an Olympic gold medal in modern history—James B. Connolly in the triple jump—was not originally selected for that group. Nowadays, universities the world over seek out and grant tempting scholarships to promising young athletes. Connolly, then a Harvard junior, asked for a leave of absence from his studies, was turned down, shrugged and paid his own way to Athens. He did turn professional some time afterward, but only as a writer.

1

2

3

At the St. Louis Games in 1904, though Cuba and South Africa were on hand, the East Coast Americans who'd ventured to Athens and then to Paris in 1900 through the Boston connection were no-shows, though members of the New York Athletic Club and other East Coast clubs participated. Gradually, however, the Games got bigger and bigger and better organized, and heroes began to emerge — in 1920, to take one illustrious year, Charley Paddock, alias the World's Fastest Human, and Paavo Nurmi, the Flying Finn. There hasn't been terribly much blood shed in actual Olympic competitions so far — though there have been heart-tugging misadventures, like the Mary Decker-Slaney — Zola Budd entanglement in Los Angeles in 1984 — but 1924 was notable as the year in which an Italian fencer, disqualified for life upon being cited for impropriety in a sabre event, challenged an

adversary to a genuine duel. "In ancient days nations stopped wars to compete in the Games," Brundage was moved to say when the 1944 Olympics were perforce canceled. "Nowadays we stop the Olympics to continue our wars."

In 1931, the I.O.C. gave the 1936 Games to Berlin. The idea apparently was to show that the rest of the world recognized that in the Weimar Republic, Germany had attained a democratic form of government and deserved to be readmitted into the fraternity of civilized nations. Then Hitler took over. Many people in other countries were for pulling out of his Olympics, and Brundage, then influential solely in American circles, went to Germany to investigate the situation and report back home. He was persuaded that the Nazis would not discriminate against any Jews, including German ones. It was perhaps fortunate for Brundage

when Hitler's master-race nonsense was soundly refuted by Jesse Owens' three triumphs over the best the rest of the world could put up against him.

In 1972, thirty-six years — seven Olympiads — later, the Olympics returned to Germany. This time, at the end of Brundage's twenty-year tenure at the I.O.C., Munich got the nod. It would be his and the world's misfortune that this was the time, too, when Palestinian terrorists murdered eleven members of the Israeli team. Brundage, three weeks from his 85th birthday, decreed that the show must go on, and of course it did.

At Mexico City in 1968, after the joyful atmosphere had been dispelled a week before the Games began when police shot and killed some demonstrating students, Brundage had produced an earlier "show-must-go-on." He had also told his I.O.C. colleagues, a bit plaintively,

1] Charley Paddock of the U.S., who won the 100 meters at the 1920 Olympics and with it the title of the world's fastest human.

2] Nadia Comaneci of Romania on her way to earning a 10 on the balance beam at the 1980 Olympics, where she won the gold.

3] Jesse Owens disproved Hitler's master race theories by winning three individual gold medals at the Berlin Games in 1936. Here he wins the long jump.

4] Paavo Nurmi, the legendary "Flying Finn," who won nine Olympic gold medals from 1920 to 1928.

5] The U.S.S.R. (in dark), which entered the Olympics in 1952, lost to the U.S. in the basketball final.

6] Wilma Rudolph overcame serious childhood illnesses, including polio, to win three gold medals at Rome in 1960.

"We are expected to settle the Chinese, South African, Korean and German problems." He had previously believed that insofar as the Olympics were concerned he had at least settled the German problem, by getting West and East Germany, from 1956 through 1964, to field a joint team, to parade behind the neutral Olympic flag, and to use for their anthem strains from Beethoven's Ninth.

Today nobody has to be reminded that the Olympic Games and politics are indivisible. Not everybody realizes that—forgetting Greece and Rome—that was the case as far back as 1908, when a Finnish team elected to parade without a flag rather than associate themselves with that of their Russian overlords. Then, to cite another of a number of instances, there was the defection from the 1976 Montreal Games of twenty-eight African nations, because some

New Zealanders had played rugby—a non-Olympic sport since 1924—in South Africa. But no amount of political intrigue can ever obscure the splendor of individual achievements, like Bob Beamon's electrifying long jump in Mexico City in 1968 or the large scale gold-mining of Carl Lewis and Mark Spitz in later Games.

Occasionally, a potentially rough situation does get smoothed out. When there was a nomenclatural change in Africa in 1964, the athletes who at the opening ceremonies represented Northern Rhodesia matter-of-factly paraded at the closing ones for Zambia. The Republic of China—Taiwan—has been in and out, chiefly to appease the People's Republic; and the two Koreas have been jousting ever since this fall's Games were awarded to Seoul. There has, though, been at least one encouraging development in this cheerless area: After the United

States boycotted the 1980 Moscow Games and the Soviet Union predictably retaliated by skipping Los Angeles the next time around, the I.O.C. banged both countries' heads together at Indianapolis in 1985 and got them to sign an "agreement of cooperation and understanding" in which they both pledged to "do their utmost to ensure that their two teams participate in the Olympic Games."

1] Women athletes have come a long way
   since the turn of the century, as these
   two photographs show. Tamara Press of
   the U.S.S.R., exhibiting the all-consuming
   intensity and power which helped her
   to dominate the women's shot put in
   the early 1960s, contrasts sharply with
2] the prim and elegant high-jump
   demonstration at the 1908 Games.

3] Every four years the Olympic torch is lit
   in Greece and brought to the Olympic
   site by several thousand runners from
   different countries. Here the torch is lit
   prior to being carried to Berlin for the
   start of the 1936 Games.

The Greeks prescribed death for any female desecrating their Olympics with her presence, and neither de Coubertin nor Brundage had much use for women as athletes. I recall hearing Brundage, at the outset of the Tokyo Games, acclaim the Olympic movement as "a Twentieth-Century religion" and ascribe to that faith the adjectives modern, exciting, dynamic — and virile. It is an irony of Olympic proportions that from 1972 to 1985 the I.O.C.'s administrative reins were in the firm grasp of a high priestess, Monique Berlioux. In an earlier incarnation, she had swum for France in the 1948 Games. By 1984, women, though deemed too frail between 1928 and 1948 to run more than one hundred Olympic meters, had a marathon of their own. Donna de Varona, the 1960-64 Olympic swimmer, has suggested that whereas Pheidippides dropped dead in 490 B.C. upon bringing

to Athens the news of the defeat of the Persians at Marathon, a woman courier might have conveyed the tidings just as readily and have survived.

Among the memorable women in Olympic annals for whom I've always had a soft spot, perhaps in part because she married a writer, Finley Peter Dunne, is Margaret Abbott. She won the gold in women's golf in Paris in 1900, although her score for nine-hole competition was a middling 47. No matter. Born in Calcutta, Miss Abbott was an artist as well as an athlete; she studied in Paris with both Degas and Rodin. She peaked too soon to have a shot at winning yet another gold in her second specialty, for art rated as a full-fledged Olympic competition only from 1912 to 1948. At Seoul the agenda calls for fifteen cultural and artistic festivals peripheral to the Games. The painters and sculptors whose works are

exhibited will not be vying for golds, silvers or bronzes, however. That's because when their fields of prowess were dropped as bona-fide Olympic events — the reasons given were that art had become too professional.

And there is hope for sports, too. There was prize money, substantial amounts of it, to be shared among the three front-runners in the competition last spring for places on the American marathon squads; but the winners said afterward that that wasn't what spurred them on: most of all, they wanted to be accorded the inestimable honor of being known as members of the United States Olympic team. ■

XXIV OLYMPIC SUMMER GAMES
SEOUL ◆ KOREA

◆ **Official 1988 U.S.A. Summer Olympic Team Print** ◆

Participate in the tremendous team effort that is necessary to send our athletes to Seoul, Korea to compete against the world. For a $25.00 tax-deductible donation you will receive the official "1988 U.S. Summer Olympic Team" print. These funds enable us to continue the excellent tradition of our Olympic athletes.

To receive your official
"1988 U.S. Summer Olympic Team" print call:

The U.S. Olympic Committee at 1-800-847-2872

ATHLETICS/TRACK

by James Dunaway

● Men	● Women
100 m.	100 m.
200 m.	200 m.
400 m.	400 m.
4 x 100 m. relay	4 x 100 m. relay
4 x 400 m. relay	4 x 400 m. relay
800 m.	800 m.
1500 m.	1500 m.
5000 m.	3000 m.
10,000 m.	10,000 m.
Marathon	Marathon
110 m. hurdles	100 m. hurdles
400 m. hurdles	400 m. hurdles
3000 m. steeplechase	
20 km. walk	
50 km. walk	

In what has been described as one of the greatest races ever, it took careful analysis of the photo finish to decide that Edwin Moses of the U.S. had beaten teammate Danny Harris (left), who won the silver, and West Germany's Harald Schmid (center) by .02 seconds in the 400-meter hurdles at the 1987 World Championships. The three will go at it again at Seoul.

The Olympic Games began with a track event. A straightaway footrace of about 200 yards was the only event of the first recorded Games at Olympia in 776 B.C. Today, nearly twenty-eight centuries later, foot racing is still the centerpiece of the Olympics.

Running itself is simple. Racing, especially at the Olympic level, is harder and more complicated than it looks. World-class track athletes often push themselves to the physical limit of their bodies, and sometimes beyond, both in racing and training. Sometimes they get away with it. Sometimes they don't, which is why so many great runners turn up injured at Olympics time.

Because the 1988 Games will be the first Olympics since 1972 in which almost all of the nations of the world will take part, you can expect to see the greatest track and field competition in Olympic history. In many events the semifinals, or even the quarterfinals, will have the quality and depth of Olympic finals in previous Games.

This year there are twenty-seven Olympic track events—fifteen men's and twelve women's. One new event, the

James Dunaway has covered hundreds of track meets for the Associated Press, *The New York Times* and numerous other publications. He is the author of *Sports Illustrated Track and Field: Running Events*.

East Germany's Silke Moller (formerly Gladisch), who won the 100 and 200 at the 1987 World Championships, will have to defeat teammate Heike Drechsler, among others, if she is to repeat at Seoul.

women's 10,000-meter run, has been added to the program for Seoul. Although they all involve footracing, by their nature they fall into several different categories.

First, there are the sprints, from 100 to 400 meters, where the only thing that counts is sheer speed. You don't worry about tactics, you just get there fast.

You do worry about technique. A good start can be vital, especially in the shortest Olympic sprint, the 100-meter dash. In last year's World Championships at Rome, Jamaica-born Ben Johnson of Canada was off to such a fast start that many observers thought he had jumped the gun. They were wrong; they were merely seeing a perfect start. The electronic starting blocks, which measure the time between the firing of the starter's pistol and the first pressure of the runner's feet against the blocks, showed that Johnson had trained his reactions to the gun so perfectly that he was simply off and running faster than anyone else—so much faster that in the first few steps he had gained a full meter lead on Carl Lewis of the United States and the rest of the field.

Lewis, who had beaten Johnson easily in the 1984 Olympic 100, ran the greatest race of his life, tying the old world record of 9.93 seconds. But Johnson's start proved decisive; he held his one-meter lead to the finish and demolished the world record by a full tenth of a second, lowering it to 9.83.

Lewis, of course, wants to repeat his Los Angeles feat of winning four gold medals. He will be heavily favored in the long jump and 200 meters, and should be able to lead the United States to another victory in the 400 relay. More than any of these, he wants to beat Johnson and win the Olympic 100 title again.

"Even though Carl ran his fastest race at Rome, it was one of his worst races ever from the point of view of his form," says Tom Tellez, Lewis' coach. "I really feel Carl should win the 100 at Seoul if he runs the race he is capable of."

With Charlie Francis, Johnson's coach, talking about a 9.75-second 100, the final promises to be quite a race.

The United States has its strongest group of female sprinters in years: not only 1984 Olympic gold medalists Evelyn Ashford and Valerie Brisco, but also a number of rapidly improving younger runners such as 21-year-old Gail Devers and 23-year-old Gwen Torrence, winners of the Pan American Games 100 and 200,

respectively. At Seoul they will challenge East Germany's longtime domination of the women's sprints. The GDR's Silke Moller (formerly Gladisch) is the favorite on the strength of her convincing victories in the 100 and 200 at the World Championships. But she'll have to run even faster in Seoul to beat the Americans.

Devers, who is also the American record holder in the 100-meter hurdles, gives

the U.S. its best chance for a medal in that event in several Olympiads.

Hurdling is defined as "sprinting over barriers." To get an idea of what it's like, imagine running full speed and every ten yards jumping over a three-drawer file cabinet (if you're a man), or an office desk (if you're a woman).

Hurdling skills are far more important in the shorter races — 110 meters for men and 100 meters for women — than in the 400. The faster the hurdler gets over the barriers (and the less time spent in the air), the faster he or she gets to the finish line. To see how good a hurdler really is, watch the lead leg as it snaps down after a hurdle clearance. If the lead foot touches the track while the trailing leg is still over the top of the hurdle, you're seeing something special.

Heike Drechsler

If you started long jumping at age twelve (perhaps your mother was a long jumper when she was a girl), and by the time you were eighteen you'd won the World Championship, what would you do for an encore? If you're Heike Drechsler, you become one of the world's great sprinters, too. So today, in addition to being the co-holder of the world long jump record (with the USA's Jackie Joyner-Kersee), Frau Drechsler is also co-holder of the world record for 200 meters. At the 1987 World Championships, Heike skipped the 200 to concentrate on the 100 and long jump; she got a poor start in the 100 and injured herself in the long jump, so she had to settle for two silver medals. Having missed the 1984 Olympics because of the Eastern Bloc boycott (she got married on the day of the opening ceremonies), will she go for the same four medals that Carl Lewis won in 1984? We won't know until September …but she reminds us, "I'm not Carl Lewis. I am Heike Drechsler."

The closest to perfection in hurdling form you're likely to see this year is that of two-time World Champion Greg Foster of Los Angeles. But Foster has a unique problem: while most high hurdlers have to extend their strides to cover the distance between successive hurdles in the necessary three steps, Foster's legs are so long that he has to shorten his stride to avoid crashing into the hurdle. It's not easy; Foster has "crashed and burned" in at least two races in each of the last four years. Foster was the Olympic favorite in 1984, but a shaky start caused him to finish second by a foot to fellow-American Roger Kingdom.

If Foster can stay on his feet in Seoul he should finally get his gold medal, but Kingdom and two other Americans, Tonie Campbell and Renaldo Nehemiah, won't leave him any margin for error.

Four-hundred-meter hurdlers don't have to be quite so skillful at skimming the barriers. The hurdles are lower—36 inches for men, 30 inches for women—and speed and strength are the keys. Neither of the 1987 World Champions, Edwin Moses of the United States nor Sabine Busch of East Germany, is a picture-book hurdler, but both have the strength to drive hard over the last two hurdles and hold their speed to the finish line.

Busch won her World Championship easily; Moses' victory at Rome was the hardest of his life. Moses, Harald Schmid of West Germany and Danny Harris of the United States raced only a yard or two apart for the final 100 meters. At the finish, all three leaned into the tape together, so close that each look at the video replay seemed to show a different winner. Finally, Moses was declared the winner by .02 of a second over Harris and Schmid. *Track and Field News* called it "one of the great footraces of all time."

Earlier in the year, Harris broke Moses' nine-year, 107-race string of consecutive victories. In Seoul, another Moses streak will be on the line: since winning the 1976 Olympic gold medal at Montreal, Moses hasn't lost a championship race of any kind, national or international.

Arguably the greatest distance runner of all time, Moroccan Said Aouita currently holds world records at 1500 and 5000 meters, and he seeks to match the legendary Paavo Nurmi's feat (1923-26) of setting every world record from 1500 to 10,000 meters.

The rematch of Moses, Harris and Schmid is probably the most eagerly anticipated of all the Seoul track events.

The middle distance races, 800 and 1500 meters, are still primarily speed- dominated races, but other factors — stamina, strategy, determination and racing ability — become increasingly important.

The glamour event, of course, is the 1500, the so-called Metric Mile. It has been described as "the perfect race: long enough for a lot of strategy and tactics, and short enough so you don't get bored."

In the longer distance races, the 3000, 5000 and 10,000, the 3000 steeplechase and the marathon, sheer speed takes a back seat to endurance, tactical skill and mental toughness. You can never get away from speed entirely, though: even marathons are sometimes won by a sprint in the final 50 meters.

The middle and long distance races at Seoul, both men's and women's, are among the most intriguing in history. The fields are studded with strong personalities.

To begin with, Mary Decker-Slaney. Since she burst into our consciousness in 1974, when as "little Mary Decker" she set a world indoor best for 880 yards at age 15, Slaney has been dogged with bad luck. A leg injury prevented her from trying for the 1976 U.S. Olympic team. In 1980, she won the Olympic Trials and broke the American 1500 record four times, but the U.S. boycott kept her out of the Moscow Games. After surgery in 1982, she set world records for the mile, the 5000 and 10,000, and in 1983 she fought off last-lap challenges by favored Soviet runners to win a brilliant double victory at 1500 and 3000 in the World Championships at Helsinki.

That disastrous collision with Zola Budd in the 1984 Olympic 3000 final cost Slaney a shot at a gold medal, but she rebounded in 1985 to lead the world rankings at 1500 and 3000. Now, after taking 1986 off to have a baby, training hard for most of 1987 and encountering a string of nagging leg injuries, she is getting ready for what may be her last chance for an Olympic medal. She should win the 3000 gold in Seoul if she can stay healthy.

Twice Britain's Sebastian Coe has gone into the Olympic Games as the world record holder in the 800 and emerged with the silver medal. Both times he came back from defeat to win the gold medal in the 1500 a few days later. No one else has ever won two Olympic 1500 gold medals.

Apart from his speed, what sets Coe apart from the ordinary multiple world record holder is the graceful elegance of his running style. It's worth looking at: he seems to flow effortlessly along the track, and hardly appears durable enough to endure the jostling and elbowing of

The brilliant world-record performance of Canada's Ben Johnson in the 100 meters at Rome, when he beat Carl Lewis with a 9.83 finish, has set the stage for an exciting rematch at Seoul. Johnson's explosive speed out of the starting blocks has his coach talking about the possibility of a 9.75-second race.

middle distance running. Yet he has been at the top for more than a decade.

Articulate as well as talented, Coe has become a spokesman for the rights of athletes, and has a full-time job as vice-chairman of the British Sports Council. Coe will celebrate his 32nd birthday during the Games, and like Slaney he was plagued with injuries in 1987. But he still holds the world record for 800, and he still wants a gold medal at his "best" distance as well as an unprecedented third 1500 gold in his last Olympic Games.

To win either the 800 or 1500 at Seoul, Coe will not only have to beat talented fellow Britishers such as Steve Cram, world record holder for the mile at 3:46:32, but a phalanx of African runners led by 800 World Champion Billy Konchellah of Kenya and 1500 champion Abdi Bile of Somalia.

Coe may also have to deal with a skinny, unpredictable Moroccan who could quite possibly turn out to be the greatest runner of all time.

His name is Said Aouita. From September 1983 to September 1987, Aouita ran more than fifty races at distances from 800 to 10,000 meters against the best runners in the world, and won all but one of them. In the race he lost, in Nice in July 1985, Aouita broke the world record in the 1500 but finished a foot behind Great Britain's Steve Cram after being obstructed by another runner in the last lap. Five weeks later in Berlin, Aouita broke Cram's 1500 record when he ran the distance in 3:29:46 and became only the fourth man in history to hold both the 1500 and 5000 world records.

Two of the races in Aouita's victory string were the 1984 Olympic 5000 and the 1987 World Championships 5000. In the Olympic race, Aouita stayed with a withering pace set by Antonio Leitao of Portugal, then accelerated devastatingly in the last half-lap to build a 10-meter margin which saw him waving to the crowd as he came down the homestretch.

After the race, a reporter asked him what would have happened if he would have entered the 1500, as he had originally indicated.

"I would have won it just as easily," Aouita answered.

Carl Lewis

After he lost to Ben Johnson in the 1987 World Championship 100-meter dash, some people wondered, "Is Carl Lewis over the hill?" But Lewis came back six days later to win easily against the best long jump field in history, then anchored the U.S. 400-meter relay team to a come-from-behind victory in 38.90 seconds, barely missing the world record. "Carl loves competition," says his coach, Tom Tellez. "And the better his competitors perform, the more he enjoys it, because it makes him perform better." For 1988, the 28-year-old Lewis is focusing more on track and field, less on show biz. Can he repeat his 1984 Olympic feat by winning four gold medals in Seoul? Obviously, beating Johnson is the key, and, says Tellez, don't give up on Lewis yet: "Carl doesn't consider himself out of the 100 meters, and I don't either. He can do anything he wants to."

At the 1987 World Championships in Rome, Aouita first announced he would try to win the 10,000 as well as the 5000. Then he said he would run only the 1500. Coming from a country with only one or two other world class runners, Aouita has the rare luxury of being named to the Moroccan team for every distance from 800 to 10,000 meters.

Eventually, Aouita decided to run only the 5000, just as in Los Angeles. The pace was slow, but the result was the same: a blazing last lap by Aouita that left the rest of the field ten meters behind. It seemed as if everyone else in the race had conceded victory to Aouita before the start and was running for second.

As one American runner said about Aouita in 1985: "You can't really say you *race* against Aouita. He dictates the race."

Aouita says he wants to match Paavo Nurmi's 1923-1926 feat of holding every world record from 1500 to 10,000, and he is halfway there. He also holds the world record for 2000 meters, has the second fastest time for the mile and 3000 meters and the seventh fastest for 10,000.

In Seoul, he will again be entered in the 800, 1500, 5000 and 10,000, and we won't know for sure what he will do until just before the competition starts. The schedule will permit him to run in either the 800 or the 10,000 in the first four days of competition, and the 1500 or 5000 in the closing days, although the 5000 heats begin just two days after the 800 final.

Whatever Aouita decides to do, it's certain to be exciting.

Two of the most wide-open men's races in Seoul are the 3000 steeplechase and the marathon. Francesco Panetta of Italy ran away with the World Championships steeplechase last fall in near world-record time and is the obvious favorite. But Panetta will find the going much tougher eight time zones away from home. He'll also face a stronger field, including 1984 Olympic champion Julius Korir of Kenya, who did not run in Rome.

If the weather is cool on October 2, you might see the fastest men's marathon in history, though the winner is almost certain to be a surprise. These days, major men's marathons are rarely won by favorites. In fact, there shouldn't be favorites: there are simply too many talented, well-conditioned athletes training for the marathon today for any valid favorite to be established.

For example, an almost unknown Kenyan named Douglas Wakihuru won the 1987 World Championships marathon. Among those he defeated were defending World Champion Rob de Castella of Australia, European champion Gelindo Bordin of Italy and World Cup champion Ahmed Saleh of Djibouti.

Even first-time marathoners have a chance. The 1984 Olympic silver medalist, John Treacy of Ireland, was running his first when he finished second to Carlos Lopes of Portugal. And three months later, running in his first marathon, Briton Steve Jones defeated Lopes — and set a then-world best of 2:08:05 while doing it.

Valerie Brisco

Valerie Brisco has had a roller coaster career in track and field since she hit the bigtime in 1979. After finishing second in the national championships 200 meters at age eighteen and fourth in the Pan American Games a year later, an injury in 1980 and the birth of her son in 1982 kept her out of the spotlight for four years. She came back strong in 1984, becoming the first American woman to break 50 seconds for 400 meters and then winning three gold medals in the Los Angeles Olympics. The American records she set in L.A. — 200 in 21.83 seconds, 400 in 48.83 and the 4 x 400 relay in 3:18:29 — still stand. She had another down year in 1987. First there was a divorce, then, in the national championships 400, Valerie ran the first half too hard and slowed at the end. She made the U.S. team for the World Championships — but only in a relay. Will she be ready for Seoul? Says Valerie, "I wasn't there in '87, but I'll be there in '88."

One who apparently will not have a chance is Belanyeh Dinsamo, who broke the world best when he ran 2:06:50 in Rotterdam earlier this year. Dinsamo's country, Ethiopia, has announced it is boycotting the Games. In that same race, however, Saleh recorded history's second fastest time, 2:07:07, and he should be a contender in Seoul.

The women's timetable at Seoul seems designed to tempt distance runners to go for a double. The marathon will be held on the first day and the 3000 final on the third. Although the 10,000 heats will start the next day, the final will not be run until five days later.

Most likely to benefit is 32-year-old Ingrid Kristiansen of Norway, who holds every women's world record from 5000 meters up and who has become the best female distance runner in the world since having a baby five years ago. Until then, Kristiansen had been only the second-best woman distance runner in Oslo, always behind Grete Waitz.

Nine days after her son was born, Ingrid was back into training, running hard. Within two years she had set world records for the 5000 and 10,000 and a world best in the marathon. She finished fourth in the 1984 Olympic marathon behind Joan Benoit (now Samuelson), Waitz and Rosa Mota of Portugal, and she lost to Benoit in the Chicago marathon in 1985. Since then she has been unbeaten in marathons and at 5000 and 10,000 meters on the track. Usually she runs alone in the lead, setting a pace so hard that other runners simply cannot keep up.

That's how Kristiansen set all her world records, and how she won the World Championship 10,000 in Rome. "We were afraid to stay with her," said one opponent.

Kristiansen has announced she will not run the marathon in Seoul but will try to double in the 3000 and 10,000. The 3000 represents a real challenge for her because she will have to beat at least five runners with much faster times than her pre-1988 best of 8:34:10, including Slaney and Maricica Puica of Romania, the 1984 Olympic champion.

Abdi Bile of Somalia will be a strong contender in the 1500, which he is seen here winning at the 1987 World Championships.

	MEN				WOMEN			
EVENT								
100m	9.83	B. Johnson	CAN	1987	10.76	E. Ashford	USA	1984
200m	19.72	P. Mennea	ITA	1979	21.71	M. Koch	GDR	1979
						H. Drechsler	GDR	1986
400m	43.86	L. Evans	USA	1968	47.60	M. Koch	GDR	1985
800m	1:41.73	S. Coe	GBR	1981	1:53.28	J. Kratochvilova	TCH	1983
1500m	3:29.46	S. Aouita	MAR	1985	3:52.47	T. Kazankina	URS	1980
3000m					8:22.62	T. Kazankina	URS	1984
5000m	12:58.39	S. Aouita	MAR	1987				
10,000m	27:13.81	F. Mamede	POR	1984	30:13.74	I. Kristiansen	NOR	1986
4x100m relay	37.83*	Graddy, Brown, Smith, Lewis	USA	1984	41.37	Gladisch, Rieger, Auerswald, Goehr	GDR	1985
4x400m relay	2:56.16*	Matthews, James, Freeman, Evans	USA	1968	3:15.92	Walther, Busch, Rubsam, Koch	GDR	1984
100m hurdles					12.25	G. Zaghorcheva	BUL	1987
110m hurdles	12.93	R. Nehemiah	USA	1981				
400m hurdles	47.02	E. Moses	USA	1983	52.94	M. Stepanova	URS	1986
Steeplechase	8:05.40	H. Rono	KEN	1978				
Marathon•	2:06:49.00	B. Densimo	ETH	1988	2:21:06.00	I. Kristiansen	NOR	1985
20km. walk	1:18:40.00	E. Canto	MEX	1984				
50km. walk	3:41:38.40	R. Gonzalez	MEX	1979				

*World record set at Olympics.   •World best, not world record

World Records (as of 6/1/88)

Douglas Wakihuru's marvelous smile at his 1987 World Championship marathon victory suggests what the joy of athletic competition is all about. Another of the great Kenyan runners, Wakihuru will be tough to beat at Seoul.

The field in the 10,000 shouldn't be as difficult for Kristiansen. Her world record in that event is 43 seconds faster than any other woman has ever run.

With Kristiansen skipping the marathon and Samuelson unable to compete due to injuries, which kept her out of the American Trials, Rosa Mota figures to have an easy time upgrading the bronze medal she won at Los Angeles. Last year Mota won the World Championship by more than seven minutes, the largest winning margin ever in a major international women's marathon.

The walks are, like the marathon, contested on the roads, and, also like the marathon, they require a long, sustained effort. But they also demand a special technique: walkers must maintain contact with the ground at all times and must straighten the knee at least momentarily on each stride, all the time racing as fast as possible. Judges watch the walkers closely; one violation brings a warning, a second or third usually means disqualification.

Kristiansen of Norway and Aouita of Morocco are examples of one of the most striking developments in track and field over the last twenty years: the emergence of smaller nations as major powers.

At the 1987 World Championships in Rome, only five countries won more than two gold medals: The United States (population 240 million) with nine, and the Soviet Union (population 280 million) with five. The other three were East Germany (population 17 million) with ten, Kenya (population 21 million) with three, and Bulgaria (population 9 million) with three.

Why do Kenya and East Germany, for example, get so much more out of their athletes than other nations several times their size? The answers are as different as the two countries and their people.

Most of Kenya's runners are members of the Kelenjin Tribe, which numbers some two million people or about 11 percent of Kenya's population. The Kelenjin live in the rolling red hills and highlands west of the Rift Valley, many at altitudes of well over a mile. The respiratory systems of people living at such high altitudes adapt by becoming better at using the limited oxygen available to them from the thin air they breathe.

Since success at distance running depends on the body's ability to use oxygen efficiently, the Kelenjin have a head start on most other runners.

That isn't their only advantage. The Kelenjin are small farmers and cattle raisers, and their children often have to travel several miles every day to get to school. Usually they run. Kipchoge Keino, the 1968 Olympic 1500 champion and 1972 steeplechase champion, used to run more than ten miles each way to get to school.

Keino's success as a runner made him a national hero in a country which had few famous men. Every Kelenjin boy wanted to grow up to be a track star, and quite a few did. In the 1968 and 1972 Olympics, in fact, Kenyans won eleven out of thirty possible medals in the five middle and long distance events—more than twice as many as any other country.

Then came the years of boycotts. One Olympic boycott is devastating enough to a country's athletes; Kenya's runners suffered through two in a row. In 1976, Kenya joined the Black African protest against New Zealand's participation at Montreal, and in 1980 Kenya joined the U.S. boycott of the Moscow Games. The most notable Kenyan casualty was Henry Rono, who in 1980 held world records in the 5000, 10,000 and steeplechase.

In 1984 at Los Angeles, the Kenyan runners made a partial comeback. They only won two men's medals—one gold and one bronze—but six others finished in fourth, fifth or sixth place. Then last year at the World Championships, Kenyans won the men's 800 (Billy Konchellah),

10,000 (Paul Kipkoech) and marathon (Wakihuru) — taking home more men's gold medals than any country except the U.S. and East Germany. All three Kenyan World Champions figure to be in Seoul, and they'll have plenty of high-caliber company. In the 1988 world cross country championships, Kenyans took eight of the first nine places, led by John Ngugi, who won his third title. He will be among the favorites in the 5000.

East Germany's success story is as man-made as Kenya's is natural. It begins with mass sports participation by and physical testing of virtually every grammar school child in the country. The testing is designed not only to uncover athletic talent, but also to indicate in which specific sport or sports each young athlete is most likely to excel.

Specialized training begins early. Typically, a 12-year-old who has potential as a sprinter may be given a chance to leave his home town to live and train in a *sporthochschule* in Leipzig, Berlin, Dresden, Potsdam or another city.

Once at the *sporthochschule*, the 12-year-old becomes part of a system that combines science, hard work and constant observation. Training activities, diet, schoolwork and competition are carefully scheduled according to the latest research conducted by the National Sports Institute in Leipzig. Progress is checked not only by time trials and competitions, but also by blood testing and other scientific analyses.

Every July, thousands of the nation's best young athletes come to East Berlin to compete in the Spartakiade, the national youth championships. This gives the young athletes experience at competing under pressure and gives the coaches and managers a chance to see how well their charges perform under championship conditions.

The close supervision continues throughout the athletes' careers — and right up to the eve of major competitions. The GDR team for the 1987 World Championships wasn't picked until the national championships, barely a week before the World Championships began, and only athletes deemed likely to win a medal were chosen for the national team.

The process seems to work. In those 1987 World Championships, the East German men and women combined to win thirteen of forty-three gold medals and 31 of a possible 129 medals overall.

If the United States and the Soviet Union could produce medal winners in the same proportion as East Germany, or even Kenya, there wouldn't be many medals left for anyone else. ■

Ingrid Kristiansen

Every day when she's at home in Oslo, Ingrid Kristiansen runs as hard as she can for 40 minutes on a treadmill in her basement. As she runs, she checks her running form in a full-length mirror on the wall in front of her. "After that, running alone against a watch is a laugh," she says. When she's away from home and racing, she runs just as hard, and almost always ends up alone. Sample 1987 trip: March 20, Adelaide, South Australia, wins 15-kilometer road racing World Championships by nearly two minutes; March 27, Auckland, New Zealand, wins cross country World Championships by nineteen seconds; April 17, wins London Marathon by five minutes. Rival runners face Hobson's choice when racing against her: they either try to keep up and risk getting run into the ground, or they let her go and give up any chance of winning. Says Ingrid, "I like to run alone."

ATHLETICS/FIELD

by James Dunaway

●**Men**
High jump
Pole vault
Long jump
Triple jump
Shot put
Discus
Javelin
Hammer
Decathlon

●**Women**
High jump
Long jump
Shot put
Discus
Javelin
Heptathlon

Track and field is a sport of running, jumping and throwing. The jumping and throwing parts are called the field events.

Although running events and field events are lumped together in a single sport, the athletes and what they do are very different.

Runners compete against each other. Field event athletes compete against a common opponent: gravity.

The runners in a race compete at the same time, running more or less together on the same track, yet as a rule they hardly know each other. A nod and a handshake before the race, a handshake to the winner after the race, are as close as they usually come. Thrown together in an Olympic village or other team situation, runners either circle each other warily or form uneasy temporary alliances, like passengers on a ship. When the meet is over, they become strangers again.

Field event athletes compete one at a time, each in turn using the same runway, landing pit or throwing circle. Their performances depend on mastering a complex technique aimed at focusing all of their strength into a single explosive burst. In that instant, a world-class jumper or thrower works harder, i.e. more intensely, than most human beings do at any time in their entire lives.

In terms of this high-intensity expenditure of effort, a field event athlete's entire competition lasts only a few seconds, though the event usually takes several hours to complete.

Rival throwers and jumpers thus spend a lot of time together when they compete and often become quite friendly. They not only lift weights, work out and socialize together, but even during competition they often help each other out with tips on technique and training.

In high-level competitions like the Olympics, of course, most athletes will try to isolate themselves from opponents and concentrate on performing well. But once the competition is over, the camaraderie returns.

Bulgarian Stefka Kostadinova more or less owns the women's high jump. Going into 1988 she had won 73 of 77 events; in addition she holds both the indoor and outdoor world records.

The Jumps

The fight to overcome gravity is most evident in the high jump and pole vault. These two events also have a common format which is different from the six other field events. Both involve getting over a bar which is raised in small increments; at each height, jumpers and vaulters have the option of competing or "passing." Of course, they only get credit for the height actually cleared, and if they miss three attempts in succession, even at different heights, they are eliminated.

Most high jumpers today use the "flop" technique, which involves going over head first, back to the bar. First to use the flop in the Olympic Games was its inventor, Dick Fosbury—it was called the "Fosbury Flop" then—and his appearance at Mexico City in 1968 caused a sensation. Today the flop is universal; the straddle technique, in which the jumper rolls over the bar face downward, is not used by any of the world's leading jumpers.

One of the strongest favorites for a gold medal at Seoul is Stefka Kostadinova in the women's high jump. The willowy 23-year-old Bulgarian looks more like a fashion model than an athlete until the jumping begins. But once it starts she is virtually unbeatable. Going into 1988, she had won a phenomenal 73 of her 77 competitions since 1985 and had accounted for 20 of the 23 jumps of 6'8¼" or higher. She rises to the occasion, too, having set world records at the indoor World Championships (6'8¾") and outdoor World Championships (6'10¼") in 1987.

"She's an extremely strong-minded girl," says America's Louise Ritter, who beat Kostadinova twice in 1987. "She jumps well even in the rain, and the only way to beat her is to jump higher. She never beats herself."

There is no such clear-cut superiority among male high jumpers, but several are flirting with eight feet. One is a long-haired, cigarette-smoking Swedish blond who gives his name as Patrik Sjoberg and his occupation as "high jumper." Like Kostadinova, Sjoberg set world indoor and outdoor records in 1987 (7'10¾" indoors and 7'11¼" outdoors), but his record in championships has been erratic. He failed to clear a height in the indoor World Championships, but then went on to win the World Championships outdoors at 7'9¾" in a thrilling contest with the two Soviet jumpers who finished 1-2 in the indoor Worlds, Igor Paklin and Gennadi Avdeyenko. One of these three ought to win at Seoul; it's hard to imagine anyone beating all three.

Incidentally, you may wonder how a jumper like Sjoberg, who jumped 7'7" or better more than thirty times in 1987 alone, can fail to clear a height altogether in some meets (it's called no-heighting). The answer is simple: since jumpers and vaulters don't have to enter the competition until they want to, many of the best ones "pass" the opportunity to jump at lower heights, partly to save energy for the really tough jumps at higher heights and partly to psyche their competition. For Sjoberg at the indoor World Championships, there was some *hubris* involved; he took his first jump in at 7'7¼". At heights like that, your technique has to be perfect; Sjoberg's wasn't.

No-heighting is more frequent in the pole vault, where wind and temperature can greatly affect a vaulter's performance. A tailwind helps the vaulter by adding to his speed as he comes down the runway. A crosswind or headwind can adversely affect both the run-up and the vault itself. Low temperatures can make the vaulter's fiberglass pole too stiff, and a hot sun can make a pole too flexible; that's one reason you'll see a vaulter put his pole away in its tubular carrying case between turns.

Even the best vaulter in the world, Sergei Bubka of the U.S.S.R., no-heights four or five times a year, usually because he is experimenting with a new pole or with starting at a very high height (say, taking his first jump at 19 feet or higher). Bubka doesn't do any experimenting in big meets, though; he just wins. Since capturing the 1983 World Championships in the rain as an unknown 19-year-old, Bubka has raised the world record by 7¾ inches (from 19'1½" to 19'9¼") and a loss to a teammate in the 1984 Friendship Games is his only defeat in a major competition.

Seeing Bubka vault is one of the great thrills of track and field. It's not just that he's by far the best in the world and possibly the best of all time. But what makes him better — superior speed, strength and technique — is startlingly evident to even the casual fan.

You do have to watch carefully to see him vault, though. Bubka usually enters the competition after everyone else and passes most heights. He took his first jump in the 1987 World Championships at 18'8¼" and won the gold medal with his second effort, at 19'2¼".

Carl Lewis of the United States is just as dominant in the men's long jump as are Kostadinova in the high jump and Bubka in the vault. Two men have jumped farther than 29 feet: 1968 Olympic champion Bob Beamon and Robert Emmiyan of the U.S.S.R., though each did it at high altitude, where lower air resistance can add six inches or more to a jump. Though Lewis has not jumped 29', he has jumped past 28'6" thirteen times, all at or near sea level, though four were wind-aided.

Lewis is favored to win both the 200 and the long jump in Seoul, especially since the International Amateur Athletic Federation revised the timetable of events for Monday, September 26. The second round of the 200 was scheduled for 2 p.m. (Seoul time) and the final of the long jump at 2:05, but after an appeal by American officials the long jump final was rescheduled for 3 p.m., giving Lewis an hour or so between the events to recover.

On the basis of his record, Lewis must be considered on a par with Jesse Owens as the greatest athlete in the history of the sport, and well ahead of him as a long jumper. From 1981 through the end of 1987, he won fifty-two straight competitions, including the 1984 Olympics, the 1983 and 1987 World Championships, and 10 indoor and outdoor U.S. and national collegiate championships. As a sprinter, he won Olympic gold medals at 100 and 200 meters and the 4 x 100 relay in 1984, plus a total of five gold medals and a silver at the 1983 and 1987 World Championships.

Robert Emmiyan of the U.S.S.R., only the second man to exceed 29 feet, will challenge Carl Lewis in the long jump at Seoul.

He is also, like Owens, a great competitor. In the 1984 Millrose Games in New York City, Lewis faced the last jump of the competition in second place behind America's Larry Myricks, the last man to beat him. Lewis needed not just a good, but a great one to beat Myricks' 27'6½", and he produced it. He leaped almost out of the landing pit with a jump of 28'10¼", which still stands as the world indoor record.

While the men's long jump is likely to be dominated by a single athlete, the women's long jump should be one of the greatest competitive events of the Games. Superathletes Jackie Joyner-Kersee of the United States and Heike Drechsler of East Germany are co-holders of the world record at 24'5½". Just behind them at 24'3" and 24'1" are Soviet jumpers Yelena Belevskaya and Galina Chistyakova.

Joyner-Kersee won the last confrontation among these four in the World Championships at Rome last September, breaking a Drechsler winning streak of twenty-seven straight. Drechsler sustained an injury on her fourth jump and eventually finished third behind Belevskaya.

Both Joyner-Kersee and Drechsler are expected to compete in other events at Seoul. Joyner-Kersee is the World Champion and world record holder in the heptathlon, which will be held the first two days of the Games, and she will come into the long jump with three full days of rest. Drechsler, silver medalist in the World Championships 100 meters and world record holder at 200, will probably run both at Seoul, although the East German coaches usually wait until the last minute before deciding who will be entered in each event. Like Lewis, Drechsler was helped by an official decision to reschedule the 200 and the long jump; the long jump final was moved from 4 p.m. to noon so that Drechsler could compete in her two best events, with the 200 semifinals at 3 p.m. and the final at 4:40. This change should give us one of the most dramatic days of the Games.

Sergei Bubka

In conversation, 24-year-old Sergei Bubka has the kind of cheerfully crafty peasant smile made famous by another Ukrainian, Nikita Khrushchev. "I'm just an ordinary guy, not Superman," Bubka says, looking you right in the eye. On the pole vault runway, he's a lot closer to Superman. His training at the Institute for Physical Culture in Donyetsk, which emphasizes weightlifting, sprinting and gymnastics, has made him the strongest, fastest pole vaulter in history. "Sergei runs as fast carrying the pole as most jumpers can run without a pole," says Soviet head coach Igor Ter-Ovanesyan. Asked how high he can jump, Bubka smiles and replies with the old Russian proverb: "First you do it, then say it." But in private, he's thinking about 6.10 meters—yes, that's 20 feet—and he'd like to do it winning the Olympic gold medal he missed because of the 1984 Soviet Olympic boycott.

Although the triple jump is contested by women in the United States at both the collegiate and national championships, it is a men-only event in the Olympics. That's a pity, because the triple jump is probably the most physically graceful of all track and field events. It's especially enjoyable to watch in slow-motion replay on television, where you can see the unique combination of strength and agility which goes into a medal-winning jump.

Still, the level of competition among the men should be exceptional. Of the thirty-one men who have hop-stepped-and-jumped farther than 57 feet, twenty-one are still competing, including ten from the Soviet Union as well as 1984 Olympic champion Al Joyner and world record holder Willie Banks of the United States.

It would not be a surprise to see Banks' world record of 58'11½" broken in the weeks leading up to the Games. The two jumpers most likely to do it are World Champion Khristo Markov of Bulgaria and the American whom Markov beat to win the Worlds, Michael Conley. Either is capable of a 59-foot jump under the right conditions; if neither does it before the Games, both might in Seoul.

The Throws

In the jumps, the athlete's body leaves the ground. In the throws, the athlete launches an implement—shot, discus, hammer or javelin—which must land within a designated area to be counted as a fair throw and measured for distance. The athlete must stay within the throwing circle or behind the scratch line while throwing or else the throw will be disqualified.

Although the techniques of throwing the implements appear relatively simple, even the simplest, putting the shot, takes years to learn to execute properly. One world class thrower, retiring at age 30 after a fourteen-year career, said plaintively, "You know, I must have thrown that damn thing ten thousand times, and I only got it really right twice!"

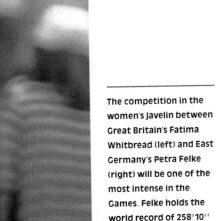

The competition in the women's javelin between Great Britain's Fatima Whitbread (left) and East Germany's Petra Felke (right) will be one of the most intense in the Games. Felke holds the world record of 258'10'' but Whitbread beat her at the most recent World Championships.

World record holder Yuri Sedykh of the U.S.S.R. will be seeking his third Olympic gold medal in the hammer throw. The only obstacle in his path should be his teammate Sergei Litvinov.

The men's shot put looks like the most wide-open field event in Seoul. Start with Switzerland's Werner Gunthor, the 1987 World Champion. Add Alessandro Andrei of Italy: although he won the 1984 Olympic gold medal over a boycott-weakened field, he set a world record, hurling the 16-pound shot 75'2'' last year and finishing second behind Gunthor in the World Championships. East Germany's 1976 Olympic champion, Udo Beyer, will be 33 in Seoul, but he threw 73'2½'' in 1987; his teammate, Ulf Timmerman, beat Gunthor to win the indoor World Championship last year but got the mumps and lost 20 pounds just before the outdoor World Championships, where he finished only fifth. He's healthy again; on May 22 Timmerman raised the world record to 75'8''. Finally, there's John Brenner, the UCLA graduate who set an American record of 73'10¾'' last year and then finished third in the World Championships.

With the exception of American Brian Oldfield, these are the five longest throwers in history. Unless one of them gets off a very long throw—72 feet or better—in the first round, it's conceivable that the lead will change hands as many as ten times during the competition.

Natalya Lisovskaya of the Soviet Union won both the indoor and outdoor World Championships last year and raised her own world record from 73'11'' to 74'3'' with the 8-pound, 13-ounce shot. She has been ranked No. 1 in the world by *Track and Field News* for the last three years, and at 26 she should be at the top of her form in Seoul. Her toughest opponent should be a fast-improving East German, Kathrin Neimke, who will be only 22. Neimke raised her personal best by five feet in 1987, from 64'6¾'' to 69'7''.

In the women's discus, the East Germans appear the strongest, having finished 1, 2, 4 in the last World Championships. An interesting question to be answered at Seoul is whether Ilke Wyludda, who at age 18 finished fourth in Rome behind countrywomen Martina Hellmann and Diana Gansky and Bulgaria's Tsvetanka Khristova, will improve enough to win the gold medal. All four threw the 2.2-pound discus 235 feet or better in 1987.

Although 21 men have thrown the discus farther than 225 feet, Jurgen Schult of East Germany became the first to do it in a major international championship when he threw the 4.4-pound discus 225'6" to win the World Championships. Why the discrepancy? Because most very long throws are aided by a wind quartering in from the throwing side, i.e. the right side for right-handed throwers, and this kind of wind is rarely found inside the large stadiums where most major championships are held. Schult's World Championships win, coupled with his world record throw of 243' in 1986 (yes, there was a strong wind that day), makes him the favorite in Seoul. John Powell, an assistant track coach at Stanford University when he's not throwing, has a history of performing well in big meets. He was third in the 1976 and 1984 Olympics, and last year, at age 40, he finished second to Schult in Rome.

As an event, the men's javelin throw is in a state of confusion. It all began on July 20, 1984, when Uwe Hohn of East Germany threw the implement 343'10" at a meet in East Berlin, breaking the

Alessandro Andrei of Italy, the 1984 Olympic gold medalist and former world record holder in the shot put, will face strong competition in Seoul from Switzerland's Werner Gunthor, the 1987 World Champion, and East Germany's Ulf Timmerman.

World Records (as of 6/1/88)								
EVENT	**MEN**				**WOMEN**			
High jump	7'11¼"	P. Sjoberg	SWE	1987	6'10¼"	S. Kostadinova	BUL	1987
Pole vault	19'9¼"	S. Bubka	URS	1987				
Long jump	29'2½"*	B. Beamon	USA	1968	24'5½"	H. Drechsler	GDR	1986
						J. Joyner-Kersee	USA	1987
Triple jump	58'11½"	W. Banks	USA	1985				
Shot put	75'8"	U. Timmerman	GDR	1988	74'3"	N. Lisovskaya	URS	1987
Discus	243'0"	J. Schult	GDR	1986	244'7"	Z. Silhava	TCH	1984
Hammer	284'7"	Y. Syedikh	URS	1986				
Javelin	287'7"	J. Zelezny	TCH	1987	258'10"	P. Felke	GDR	1987
Decathlon	8847 pts.*	D. Thompson	GBR	1984				
Heptathlon					7158 pts.	J. Joyner-Kersee	USA	1986
*World record set at Olympics								

world record by more than 16 feet. That convinced the elders of the International Amateur Athletic Federation to redesign the javelin before someone in the stands got killed. The redesign moved the center of gravity forward so that the new javelin, introduced on April 1, 1986, noses down sooner and flies a shorter distance (the record for the current javelin is 287'7"). Many throwers are still learning how to throw the new one, which is much less aerodynamic than the previous model (the old javelin, if thrown just so, would become an airfoil and "take off," adding extra yards to the throw). The World Championships witnessed a seesaw competition where the lead changed hands six times; the Olympics will probably be more of the same, with either Viktor Yevsyukov of the U.S.S.R., Jan Zelezny of Czechoslovakia, Tom Petranoff of the United States or '87 World Champion Sappo Raty of Finland most likely to emerge the winner.

The women's javelin is shorter and lighter than the men's implement, and it hasn't needed to be redesigned. Last year only two women threw it more than 230 feet—Petra Felke of East Germany, the world record holder at 258'10", and Fatima Whitbread of Great Britain, who beat Felke in the World Championships with a toss of 251'5". These two are in a class by themselves; the air is electric when they compete against each other, and it almost certainly will be in Seoul.

Like the triple jump and the pole vault, the hammer throw is an all-male event in the Olympics—and it will probably remain all male in the foreseeable future. It will probably remain all-Soviet, too; only five men have thrown the 16-pound hammer farther than 272 feet, and all are from the U.S.S.R. Soviet hammer throwers swept the medals at the 1976 and 1980 Olympics and went 1-2 in the 1987 World Championships despite the absence of Yuri Syedikh, the world record holder (284'7") and two-time Olympic champion. Syedikh was taking it easy in 1987 while getting ready to go after his third Olympic gold medal, and so fellow-Soviet Sergei Litvinov had an easy time winning the World Championship. Only Litvinov, whose best throw is 282'3", stands between Syedikh and the gold at Seoul, and their one-to-one battle, like that between Fatima Whitbread and Petra Felke, should be one of the high points of the Games.

Tom Petranoff

One day in 1977, walking away from a baseball tryout at Palomar Community College near Los Angeles, 19-year-old Tom Petranoff saw a javelin thrower practicing. It looked interesting, so Petranoff tried a couple of throws. Before he knew it, he was on the track team. Five months later he was on the U.S. national team, throwing against the Soviet Union's best (he finished second). In 1983, he set a world record of 327'2"; favored to win the Olympics the next year, he blew up and finished tenth. Today, he says, "I'm a born-again javelin thrower. I'm mellower; I've changed my style to emphasize consistency instead of power. I'm competing less, too—once every three or four weeks instead of once or twice a week. I've never had as much to prove as I do now. I had it handed to me in 1984. Now that I'm the underdog you'll see a different person."

Jackie Joyner-Kersee

Once when Jackie Joyner was a girl growing up in one of East St. Louis' toughest neighborhoods, she saw a man shot dead in front of her house. Now she's a World Champion and record holder, but she hasn't forgotten where she came from: she earmarks part of her earnings to support recreation centers like the one that got her interested in sports and kept her off the streets. Sometimes, especially when she's working on her long jump technique, her coach and husband, Bobby Kersee, yells at her. "I don't holler back," she says. "It wouldn't look good in front of the other girls on the team, so I just mutter at him under my breath. Then Bobby and I will talk about it and resolve it while we're driving home. Sometimes, after he looks at my workout on the VCR, he'll say, 'You're right.' But the arguments always stop at the front door."

Decathlon/Heptathlon

The decathlon (for men) and the heptathlon (for women) combine running, jumping and throwing events in the most taxing of track and field competitions. They are true tests of talent, versatility, stamina and determination. In Seoul, two of the greatest multi-event athletes of all time, and two of the most attractive people in the sport, are expected to dominate their respective events: Daley Thompson of Great Britain in the decathlon and American Jackie Joyner-Kersee in the heptathlon.

The ten events in the decathlon are: first day, 100-meter dash, long jump, shot put, high jump, 400-meter dash; second day, 110-meter high hurdles, discus, pole vault, javelin throw, 1500-meter run.

Thompson, born in London of a Nigerian father and a Scottish mother, has a wisecracking manner that belies his fierce desire—nay, need—to win. After winning the gold medal at Los Angeles in 1984, he donned a t-shirt with the message, "Thanks, America, for a Good Games and a Great Time," on the front, and on the back, "But What About the TV Coverage?" He describes himself as, "short, squat and ugly," and defines the decathlon as, "A year of training for about sixteen minutes of serious competition."

Last year, after winning nine major decathlons in a row since 1978, Thompson came into the World Championships (which he had won in 1983) suffering from a painful groin muscle pull and finished ninth. The winner was East Germany's 24-year-old Torsten Voss, who became the seventh-highest scorer in history with a steady, no-mistakes performance. After winning, Voss sought out Thompson and raised the Briton's arm to share the victory. He said, "I won, but Thompson remains the greatest. He could have quit but he continued right to the end. It was extraordinary."

When Thompson won his first Olympic gold medal, at Moscow in 1980, he said he hoped to eventually win five of them. Only injury—and perhaps Torsten Voss—stands between him and No. 3 in Seoul.

The women's equivalent of the decathlon, the heptathlon, consists of seven events: first day, 100-meter hurdles, discus throw, high jump, shot put, 200-meter dash; second day, long jump, javelin throw, 800-meter run.

In terms of all-around athletic ability, Jackie Joyner-Kersee is probably even more gifted than Daley Thompson—and even more dominant in the heptathlon than is Thompson in the decathlon.

Talent runs in her family. On the same day she finished second by five points to Glynis Nunn of Australia in the 1984 Olympic heptathlon—6,390 to 6,385—her brother, Al Joyner, won the gold medal in the triple jump.

Less than two years after that Olympic defeat, she broke the world record by 202 points at the Goodwill Games in Moscow. Her 7,148-point score in Moscow was the first ever over 7,000; a month later she raised the record to 7,158 in Houston.

Jackie's victory in the 1987 World Championships heptathlon underlined her total superiority in the event. Her margin of victory, 564 points over the best heptathletes in the world, was the largest ever in a major heptathlon. Three days later she tacked on an exclamation point by winning a second gold medal in the long jump, with a jump less than four inches under her own world record.

Undefeated in the heptathlon since 1984 and voted female athlete of the year two years in a row by *Track and Field News*, Joyner-Kersee is still motivated by her 1984 Olympic loss. Says her coach and husband, Bob Kersee, "I hope she gets that gold medal in 1988. If she does, then I won't have to live another four years with this obsession." ∎

Daley Thompson

If, as Daley Thompson says, the decathlon is an art, he is its Michelangelo. He has won more major decathlons—two Olympics, one World Championship, two European and three Commonwealth titles—than anyone in history. Thompson was a schoolboy sprinter until he tried his first decathlon; when he won it with a score 2000 points better than any British 16-year-old had ever done, he knew he had found his calling. He has given it his full attention ever since, working out seven or eight hours a day (less on Christmas Day, but he still trains), and talking and thinking about the ten events when he's not actually doing them. In 1987 he was voted Britain's most popular athlete. One reason is his wit: when a rival declared he would win the gold medal at Los Angeles, Daley shot back, "He'll have to steal mine or switch to another event."

CYCLING

by Bjarne Rostaing

●**Men**
Individual road race
Road team time trial
4000 m. individual pursuit
4000 m. team pursuit
One km. time trial
50 km. points race
1000 m. match sprint

●**Women**
Individual road race
1000 m. match sprint

The popularity of cycling spread quickly after the modern bicycle was developed in the 1880s. However, only within the past fifteen to twenty years has the sport achieved a truly international competitive excellence, with outstanding racers emerging from Tokyo to Bogota. In the 1976 Olympics at Montreal, a United States roadman remained with

....

Bjarne Rostaing, a former competitor who has written for *Sports Illustrated, Outside* and many cycling journals, is co-author of the *Bill Walton Total Book of Cycling* (1984).

the leaders on the cold rain-slick hills of the difficult Mount Royal course. The unexpected sixth place finish of Californian George Mount gave notice that the Americans were beginning to challenge the dominance of the Western European and Eastern Bloc powers. Eight years later, the United States took a startling nine medals.

Modern cycling is a diverse sport, ranging in distance from a single kilometer to as many as 200, covering both team and individual events and including races against opponents and against the clock. Speeds upward of 60 kilometers per hour make aerodynamic considerations critical.

Wind resistance dictates tactics based on the "draft effect," in which riders behind the leader conserve energy by following in the leader's slipstream. The decision to break away or move to the front involves accepting the handicap of confronting wind resistance, and in sprint situations riders "slingshot" from another's draft as do stock car racers.

Aerodynamics have also made cycling equipment-intensive, especially in time trials, where streamlined helmets, Lycra skinsuits and futuristic "funny bikes" are

employed to reduce drag. These are delicate, ultra light, highly specialized machines made of space-tech composites and alloys. Equipped with spokeless disc wheels and exotic components, they cost as much as some automobiles.

There are two kinds of races: road and track. Track racing is run on velodromes (banked oval tracks) whose standard Olympic dimension is 333⅓ meters with a maximum banking of 30 degrees. The track bicycle is especially adapted to this environment—brakeless, with a fixed gear that allows no freewheeling (coasting). The shortness of track events (only one is longer than four kilometers) requires a strong, quick athlete.

The road rider, by contrast, is often slight of build but with great stamina and cardiovascular capacity. And unlike some of the space-age track machines, the road bicycle is conventional in design, built to handle well under all conditions, with rim brakes and up to sixteen gears.

The road race is the queen of cycling events, the one on which major careers are built. It is a mass-start race of 196.8 kilometers for men and 82 for women raced by four-rider teams in a field of about 150. The race lasts between four and five hours for men and two to three for women, and the first rider across the line wins, requiring that a team subordinate itself to the success of one member.

Good road racing is full of "attacks"—attempts by riders to break away from the pack. Early breaks are chased down and new ones form. Tires pop and riders crash, but wheels and bikes are quickly replaced by mechanics in equipment vans. If the pack arrives together, the final meters of a road race often develop into a wild, awesome and quite dangerous "field sprint"—a huge mass of riders all jammed together, flat out in top gear, heads down, elbows banging, lungs burning.

Strategy in this race involves a complexity not found elsewhere: with thirty or more teams in contention, opponents become allies. A Soviet, a Colombian, an American and an Italian may work together in a break, because this is how the race is won. Inevitably these alliances blow apart, but their existence is at the heart of the event. While the men's race on the pancake-flat course of Seoul has no clear favorite, America's Rebecca Twigg, runaway Pan Am victor and an Olympic silver medalist in 1984, should challenge three-time World Champion Jeannie Longo of France for the gold.

In contrast to the tumultuous mass-start road race, teams of four start the team time trial at two-minute intervals then work as a unit to complete the 100-kilometer road course. Drafting in the slipstream of another team is prohibited. Only three team members need finish, and the third rider's time is the team's time. The best 100-kilometer riders tend to be big and strong, capable of sustained speeds in the 50 km./hr. range.

Although good time-trialers can look like preset robots following the coach's schedule, as they pass through phases of weakness they will often be allowed to skip their turn at the front. Often a rider too weak to lead the pack early in the race will come back strong toward the end. Another rider may power the team through the first half of the race and then drop out as the others continue. He gets his medal anyway, should his team win.

While some riders still "double" road race and time trial, the latter has become more and more specialized. The World Champion Italians and silver medalist Soviets appear the stongest here.

The gut-wrenching one-kilometer time trial on the track lasts barely a minute but is the supreme pain event in cycling. It is a simple race: there are no qualification heats, and each rider has just one

Requiring both a tactical sense and explosive sprinter's speed, the match sprint is one of cycling's most exciting events. Here 1987 World Champion Lutz Hesslich of East Germany races to the finish below the red line in the 1986 World Championships.

Teams of four compete in the 100-kilometer team time trial. The third rider across the finish line determines the time of each team, so efficient teamwork is necessary in this demanding road event.

chance. Riders go virtually flat-out from a standing start, making the kilo in essence a sprint inhumanly extended. The moment of truth comes on the final lap, when the rider reaches the limit of human ability to continue anaerobic (non-oxygen-based) effort.

This hyper-intense activity can be sustained for only about 40 seconds, and the final half-lap of a good run becomes true agony. Forcing the body beyond its capabilities has severe effects on body chemistry, causing the blood to silt with pain-causing lactic acid. Muscles turn to cement, lungs burn, vision tunnels and grays. World Champion Martin Vinnicombe of Australia will have to meet the challenge of East Germany and the Soviet Union if he is to win the gold.

Tricky, violent and sometimes dangerous, the match sprint could not be more different from the kilometer time trial, though the distance is the same. The clock means nothing in a match sprint—getting across the finish first is how you win. The result is a tactical duel that can suddenly explode into a highly physical man-to-man confrontation.

Riders proceed from a hand-held start and the pace is deceptively subdued, a cat-and-mouse game. Often the riders weave up and down the banking at walking speed, seeking positional advantage. The rear position is favored by many because the opponent is in clear view and they can ride in the draft. In the duel for position, riders may simply come to a "sur-place" (dead stop). They can hold this as long as they like, so long as they don't move backward 20 centimeters, in which case they are required to proceed, thus being forced into the lead. Sometimes a pair of riders in sur-place will stare at each other for 30 seconds or more, their bikes almost motionless.

Often things don't break loose until the final 200 meters. At this point, the lead rider can choose either the short, narrow route below the red line on the track, where he must remain, or the much wider, steeply banked upper section. The following rider may go anywhere, but if the leader is below the red line, his opponent may not chop down in front of him. When the leader stays in the lane below the red line, the finish is swift and relatively simple. The purest sprinters can jump out of the leader's draft and win at the last moment with a final explosive burst lasting only seconds. Up on the banking, though, the leader may be able to negate the following rider's speed by skillful (and legal) blocking. East Germans Lutz Hesslich, Michael Huebner and Bill Huck were 1-2-3 in the 1987 World Championships, but U.S. Pan Am winner Ken Carpenter or 1984 Olympic Champion Mark Gorski, also of the U.S., might break through. World Champion Erika Salumiae of the Soviet Union, Christa Rothenburger of East Germany, who won a gold medal in speedskating at the Calgary Winter Games, and Connie Young of the U.S. are the best women.

The 4000-meter individual pursuit has characteristics of both a time trial and a race. Two riders start on opposite sides of the track; the first to complete 4000 meters or overtake his opponent wins. Competition begins with a solo time-trial seeding of eight qualifiers, who subsequently race against each other. The fastest qualifiers are paired with the slowest. They ride on a "schedule" and are coached from trackside, though they can see each other as well. Sometimes a rider is overtaken, but usually the clock decides who wins. Winning heats by a small but safe margin saves strength for those that follow. Because of the distance and the five heats required to win, speed and stamina are both critical, and the pursuiter exists, in a sense, on the margin between road and track types. Australian World Champion Dean Woods and several Soviets are favored. Argentinian Pan Am Games victor Gabriel Curuchet could also surprise.

The 4000-meter team pursuit event is similar to the 100-kilometer (road) team time trial, with teams of four working together against the clock, but it is raced on the track, pursuit-fashion. Three members must finish, and the third rider's time is the team's time. Sustained speed, cooperation and finesse are the basic ingredients, as riders take their turns at the lead. Intricate teamwork is required to exchange positions smoothly in an

Rebecca Twigg, America's silver medalist in the 1984 Games, represents the best hope for a U.S. gold in the women's road race.

event in which tenths of a second are critical. The closer the bicycles, the more aerodynamic the team performance. Part of the art is taking one's pull at the front without a jerky acceleration that can disrupt the team's rhythm. Cool skill and fierce intensity make this the most beautiful and hypnotic of cycling events. The Soviet Union, East Germany and Czechoslovakia were 1-2-3 at the 1987 World Championships and are the teams to beat.

The 50-kilometer points race is a mass-start track event which superficially resembles a road race on the track, but is very different. Two-man teams earn points in a series of sprints which come at five-kilometer intervals. If there are no breakaways, the race tends to proceed in surges followed by calmer periods. Each sprint yields five, three, two and one points for first, second, third and fourth places; mid-point and final sprints are worth double points. In the case of a tie, the rider who places higher in the final sprint wins.

Points racing mixes sprint and pursuit riders, each with a favorite scenario: pursuiter types prefer to form a break (thus guaranteeing themselves points in each sprint), while sprinters prefer to sit in the draft of the pack (or break), jumping out to score at the last moment. Keeping track of points is essential. The Soviet Union took first in the 1987 World Championships. Two-time World Champion Leonard Harvey Nitz of the U.S. is master of the points race; given the right partner he could medal. ■

FENCING

by Jack Keane

● *Men*
Individual foil
Individual épée
Individual saber
Team foil
Team épée
Team saber

● *Women*
Individual foil
Team foil

Mathias Gey of West Germany (left), the 1987 World Champion in foil, prepares to defend against Italy's Andrea Borella in the 1984 Olympic Games. Gey, who won the silver at Los Angeles, is a powerful contender for the gold medal at Seoul.

The next time the classic film *Scaramouche* is listed for late-night TV, stay up and tune in for an excellent introduction to the fencing events at Seoul.

Early in the film, Stewart Granger, his young friend killed by the murderous French count, Mel Ferrer, grabs his friend's sword and begins slashing at the count, a master swordsman.

Effortlessly, disdainfully, Ferrer blocks each of Granger's many wild swings as he lectures him on his dead friend's folly.

....

Jack Keane, a former Pan Am Games saber champion and an Olympian in 1968 and 1972, is the only man ever selected to captain three U.S. Olympic fencing teams.

Aficionados of the sport will recognize in Ferrer's well-coached swordplay expert use of the "wall of steel" concept, the ability of a slim rod of metal—properly placed in key positions—to block an opposing blade, no matter how savagely wielded. General audiences sense that there is something more to swordsmanship than strength or aggression—technique is paramount.

At the heart of this technique is strong defense. In fact, in French, the international language of the sport, the word for fencing is "escrime," derived from the Sanskrit term "skrimmer" meaning defense.

China's Luan Jujie, the 1984 Olympic champion, will have to defeat strong fencers from West Germany and Romania if she is to win her second consecutive gold medal.

Regarded as the fastest combat sport in the world, fencing calls upon lightning reflexes, intelligence and problem-solving abilities in order to "hit without being hit."

The three traditional weapons of foil, épée and saber are still employed, though the first two have been modified to permit electronic scoring.

Men compete in all three weapons, women use only the foil.

Depressing the spring-loaded point on the end of a foil or épée blade causes an electronic scoring machine to signal a hit. In épée, hits may be scored anywhere on the body. In foil, the target is restricted to a metallic vest covering the fencer's torso.

Sabreurs may score with the point and also the cutting edge of the saber. The target is any part of the body from the hip lines up, reflecting the vulnerable areas of horsemen fighting from the saddle.

Fencers fight within an area called the "piste." For saber and épée this is a field two meters wide by eighteen long; for foil it is two meters shorter. Competitors receive a warning when they near the rear limit. If a fencer crosses the rear limit with both feet after a warning, a penalty touch is awarded even if an actual touch hasn't been scored. (Think of it as Mel Ferrer being forced over a cliff's edge.)

Beside the contestants, the most important person on the field of play is the chief judge, called the president of the jury. In foil and épée, the president usually works alone, awarding touches with the aid of the electronic scoring machine. In saber, four judges help signal touches on the valid target.

The task of each fencer is to penetrate the defense of the other with a thrust or cut. In the qualifying round-robin bouts, a competitor must score five touches to win. In the direct-elimination phase following the round-robin bouts, men must score ten touches and women must score eight. The time limit is six minutes for five touches, eight minutes for eight and ten minutes for ten-touch bouts. Should time expire, the fencer who is ahead wins. Fencers are eliminated if they lose twice in the direct elimination bouts.

In foil and saber, the rules favor the fencer who is first to extend the weapon arm and threaten the opponent's valid target. This establishes the "right of way" to attack. The opponent thereby is obliged to defend. After blocking (parrying) the attack, the defender has the right to return the thrust (riposte). Thus, the orderly sequence is attack-parry-riposte. If the original attacker parries the riposte, he or she can deliver a counter-riposte.

It is up to the president of the jury to establish the sequence of these rapid actions, which often occur in less than 1/25th of a second. The president's judgment is final.

In épée, however, the action is different. The épée is the modern version of the dueling sword, and reflects real combat. Unlike foil and saber, the rules allow épéeists to score simultaneous hits. They are not bound by the rules of "right of way" as in foil and saber; they try to hit first without being hit.

The Soviets are traditionally the strongest men's team, but they have clearly slipped in recent years. At last year's World Championships, for example, though they won team events in saber and épée, the Soviets won just one silver in the individual weapons. West Germans took the foil and épée and the French the saber.

It is possible the Soviets will again have difficulty in the Olympics, with West Germany's Mathias Gey in the foil and Volker Fischer in the épée, along with France's Jean François Lamour and Hungary's Imre Gedovari in the saber strong bets for the gold.

In women's team fencing, the West Germans are favored if they get leadership from Anje Fichtel, the 1986 World Champion who runs hot and cold. Hungary is the current title holder. For the women's individual gold, watch also for Romania's Elisabeta Tufan, 1987 World Champion, and China's Luan Jujie, the Olympic champion at Los Angeles.

Post Script: Granger escapes the count, seeks out the count's fencing master; improves miraculously; becomes Scaramouche; gives the count his come-uppance in a spectacular duel. Finis. ■

GYMNASTICS

by Kent Hannon

Shown here performing on the pommel horse, Valeri Liukin is the 1987 Soviet and European all-around champion. If he manages to complete at Seoul the triple somersault in floor exercise, which he has been working on for several years, he will become the first person in history to throw this successfully in competition.

T he 1984 Olympics were a boon to nearly every phase of America's amateur athletic program, at least in terms of the number of medals won. And nowhere do memories of Los Angeles burn brighter than in the U.S. gymnastics community, which took the fullest possible advantage of the Soviet-led boycott.

In the team competition, the American men won their first-ever gold medal and the women their first silver. In the all-around competition, Mary Lou Retton made history with a gold as did Peter Vidmar with his silver. In the individual event finals, the U.S. got medal-winning performances from Retton, Vidmar and five others.

The total of all this unprecedented winning, which took place in Hollywood's backyard with millions of Americans watching extensive coverage on television, was to give the appearance that the U.S. had finally arrived as a world gymnastics power. But four years later, with the Soviet men heavy gold medal favorites and the Soviet and Romanian women a cut above the rest of the world, the major gymnastics story in Seoul figures to be "What happened to the Americans?"

For the fact is, the U.S. is not expected to do well at Seoul. Neither the men's nor women's programs have managed to achieve real international distinction since Los Angeles.

Although the U.S. women performed admirably in nearly upsetting the perennial power, Romania, at Los Angeles, they have since finished sixth in both the 1985 and 1987 World Championships, the two principal tests for evaluating what might happen at Seoul.

And the U.S. men have not even done that well, finishing ninth in the same two competitions. The 1987 World Championships at Rotterdam looked as if it might be a turning point for the men, even though one member of the team, UCLA's Curtis Holdsworth, was competing out-

Kent Hannon, a former staff writer at *Sports Illustrated* who co-authored an award-winning book on gymnastics with Kurt Thomas, teaches journalism at the University of Georgia.

side the U.S. for the first time. But U.S. expectations were dashed by injury and near tragedy. Scott Johnson injured his foot in a warmup meet, and Tim Daggett actually flirted with death when he shattered his leg in two places during team optionals. He lost two quarts of blood before medics could get him out of the arena.

Both American teams will be relatively inexperienced in Seoul. None of the women from L.A. is still competing, and with Daggett's career in jeopardy, Johnson may be the only team member with Olympic experience.

The fallout since L.A. has U.S. Gymnastics Federation officials extremely worried.

"There's no question that Los Angeles was an unrealistic view of where we stood internationally," says Greg Marsden, the U.S. women's coach at the 1987 World Championships, who claims he'll be "surprised if the American public isn't extremely disappointed with where we're

Silver medalist to Aurelia Dobre at the 1987 World Championships, Soviet Elena Shoushounova excels in the floor exercise and the vault.

going to finish in Seoul."

A recent editorial written by Mike Jacki, executive director of the USGF, attributes some of our troubles to the athletes themselves. Jacki suggests that some U.S. athletes "lack the desire to be great," and goes on to argue that American gymnastics suffers as well because the coaches in the sport—in particular, the women's coaches, who make their living by running their own private clubs—don't take risks.

"Most of our top ten girls never compete outside the country," says Jacki. "Why? Because 95 percent of their coaches own their own clubs, and they don't want them to go overseas and get beat."

It doesn't look good, therefore it's not good for business, says Jacki, who notes that Retton's victory in Japan's Chunichi Cup was her only victory of note outside the U.S. She retired as one of the least-tested Olympic champions of all time. Lack of international experience is particularly detrimental in gymnastics because gaining clout overseas against the best in the world is the only way a Western gymnast can survive amidst the Cold War of international judging—where scores are frequently inflated or sabotaged according to whom the gymnast's country is aligned with in world politics.

Independent of the political leanings of the judges, there are several extraordinary athletes competing who should excel under any circumstances. Perhaps the strongest gymnast in the world is Dimitri Bilozertchev of the Soviet Union, who won eight gold and four silver medals in the 1983 and 1987 World Championships. Bilozertchev should be an inspiration to Daggett. He has returned, Phoenix-like, to the top of the sport after breaking his leg in forty places in a car accident one week prior to the '85 World Championships. "There was even a moment, very severe, when doctors were talking about amputation," says Bilozertchev, who will be seeking his first Olympic medals in Seoul.

The Soviets also have high hopes for Valeri Liukin, who won both the Soviet and European all-around titles in 1987. Liukin's courage in attempting a triple

Li Ning of the People's Republic of China, vaulting in the 1984 Olympics, was the bronze medalist in rings at the 1987 World Championships. He hopes to defeat the top Soviet men at Seoul.

somersault in floor exercise, and his talents away from the arena—he's a gifted skier, skateboarder and disco dancer—have made him a teen idol in the U.S.S.R.

Among the women, Aurelia (the new Nadia) Dobre, the latest Romanian star, is the most heralded. Inevitably compared to the great Nadia Comaneci, the young Romanian who electrified the gymnastics world at the 1976 Olympics when she won three gold medals, the unabashed Dobre commented, after winning the all-around medal as a fourteen-year-old at the Rotterdam World Championships, "I think Nadia is very happy today because a new Nadia is born." And then, as if to emphasize her lack of reverence for the achievements of Ms. Comaneci, she added, "In fact, I think we have six Nadias on our team."

In addition to strong performers like Elena Shoushounova, Svetlana Baitova and Oksana Omelianchik, the Soviets also have a sleeper who could capture the hearts of the spectators and judges. She is Aleftina Priakhina, a sixteen-year-old, 68-pound wonder from Ashkabad, near Iran, who finished third in the all-around at the '87 Soviet national championships.

It's important to remember that unlike any other physical discipline in the world of sport, gymnastics is constantly shedding its skin to accommodate more and more difficulty. For example, Liukin's triple somersault in floor exercise may or may not be ready for prime time. But if he throws it and nails it in the Olympic Games, everybody else will feel the pressure to come up with a triple, too. In the last few years, one-arm giant swings and release moves on high bar have been all the rage among the men. Now the women have started doing them on the uneven bars.

Only in gymnastics would you find a category—"D" Moves—where judges have to quantify how much courage it took for a gymnast to attempt a certain trick. To appreciate the skill of the participants, it's necessary to know something about the events.

The crowd's favorite, floor exercise is a source for most of the movements and disciplines found in the six men's and four women's events. Within the confines

Aurelia Dobre

Her name was Nadia, and back in the 1976 Olympics we fell in love with her, even though she was Romanian, because she was perfection, and because she reminded us of a princess in a fairy tale.

This time, her name is Aurelia, and she's going to make Americans fall in love all over again.

Aurelia Dobre is only fifteen, but she already holds thousands of Europeans' hearts hostage, thanks to her performance at the 1987 World Championships where, by scoring a 10 on the floor exercise and then winning the all-around with another 10 on the vault, she helped the Romanians upset the Soviets in the team title.

And Dobre didn't look like a machine in doing so. On her graceful, fully-extended split leaps, she resembled an apprentice at the Kirov Ballet. When she mounted on floor with a double-twisting punch front, she looked like a member of an acrobatic team.

"I will come into the Olympic Games stronger than Nadia was," said Dobre, sounding like...well, a princess.

of a 12 x 12-meter mat made of springs, wood, foam and carpet, the judges want to see everything a gymnast can do — tumbling, balance, control, technique, flexibility, flips — as well as strength (men) and dance (women).

And gymnasts have nothing to hang onto out there but air.

Despite a lot of similarities, men's floor-ex is almost a different event than the women's because of the prejudice against dance or dance-like movements on the men's side and the demand for them on the women's.

In contrast to the dance-oriented sequences of the women, men's floor-ex is a brazen display of power and athletic ability, performed without musical accompaniment.

The women are required to show creative and dynamic changes in rhythm and energy, plus a variety of acrobatic movements: tumbling, jumps, pirouettes, spins and dance. Music is an integral part of their routines, and their style and the way they display their expressions and flexibility generally correspond to the music they choose.

Dobre and Daniela Silivas of Romania, both extraordinary in the floor exercise,

do double layout back flips followed immediately by a "punch front" — a dramatic, bounce-back front somersault done so quickly after the double layout that it appears as if their coach has pushed the rewind button and sent the routines in reverse.

The pommel horse, dead last in aesthetic movements, spectacular dismounts and standing ovations from the crowd, is frequently also the most deadly because it's so easy for a gymnast to get his legs tangled up in the pommels or to fall completely off the apparatus.

The physical nature of this event — asking a man to support all his weight on his hands while he swings his legs around the horse in lateral circles, thus interfering with his hands' support position every half-second or so — seems to ask the impossible.

Phoebe Mills

If America wins a gymnastics medal in Seoul — and that's a very iffy proposition — it's likely to come from a serious-minded, all-around athlete named Phoebe Mills, who holds an international age-group record in speed skating, qualified as a Junior Olympian in diving and once played on her mom's softball team.

"She's a kid in charge, never running away from a defeat, from a difficult skill, from the pain of a hard workout," says Mills' coach, Bela Karolyi, who watched with delight as the 15-year-old put together four near-perfect routines to beat the No. 2 Russian, Svetlana Baitova, at the recent McDonald's American Cup.

"I stayed with gymnastics because there are so many sacrifices and I realized I could only commit myself to one sport," says the 4'11", 85-pound Mills.

In addition to her abundant talent, Mills is a Scorpio, and that's a good omen, according to Karolyi.

"They make good gymnasts," he says. "Nadia is a Scorpio. All my best gymnasts have been."

The secret to success on the horse is balance, and in order to score points a gymnast must keep his legs absolutely straight with toes pointed at all times. Keep your eyes peeled for two things — a move called the "Thomas Flair," which includes a series of sweeping, windmill-like leg maneuvers, and a handstand somewhere in the routine.

Watch also for Valentin Mogilnyi of the U.S.S.R. who can travel backward from one end of the horse to the other without using the pommels for leverage or balance. It doesn't look as flashy as the release moves on the high bar, but until you've tried it, you can't believe how hard it is.

More treacherous than even the pommel horse, the four-inch wide balance beam for women is usually the path either to victory or defeat in the women's all-around and team competition simply because it's so easy to fall off.

On this narrow surface, which is four feet off the floor, sixteen feet long and scarcely wider than a gymnast's foot, judges want to see tumbling (with and without flight), strength and balance moves, and dance (turns, leaps and body waves).

Elements that receive extra points from the judges include vault-like mounts onto the beam, one-arm handstands and somersaults in the midst of the routine, and double-back somersaults on the dismount.

Omelianchik does back flips with such height that her landing can make the apparatus and floor rumble.

Strictly an event for blacksmiths back when every routine was crammed full of strength moves known as "crosses," the rings have become much more interesting to watch because the emphasis has changed to include more maneuvers such as a "shoot" to a handstand.

But the crosses — those frozen, mid-air poses, complete with bulging muscles and steel-eyed stares — are still around, and the best gymnasts will show the judges several different varieties.

Yuri Korolev of the Soviet Union does an inverted cross, meaning he hangs upside down with his arms out to the sides and his toes pointed toward the ceiling. And he doesn't move. Then he bails out of it, loops down and swings right back up into another inverted cross in case you missed the first one.

The most important challenge for a gymnast here is to keep the rings from moving, thus proving he has enough strength and technique to control the ten feet of cable to which the rings are attached.

Thanks to the torque the gymnasts can produce on these long cables, the dismounts are always spectacular.

The vault is performed on the "long horse," which is a bareback version of the pommel horse. Gymnasts sprint toward the apparatus at top speed, land with

Dimitri Bilozertchev

The date was Oct. 13, 1985. Having just signed the papers which would permit him to marry, the Soviet Union's Dimitri Bilozertchev, the reigning king of gymnastics, was going out to celebrate in his father's car.

He didn't get far. Losing control in a heavy rain, he crashed into a pole, shattering his leg in forty places and breaking his hand.

Specialists were brought in and Bilozertchev underwent three operations. As soon as he could, he was back working out. During the time he was unable to put weight on his leg or risk landing on it, coaches, trainers and teammates took turns hoisting him onto the various apparatuses so he could work his hands, arms and upper body and, more importantly, keep his mind in shape.

Bilozertchev's reward came at the World Championships in Rotterdam last October when he won the all-around competition.

How did he do it?

"You must want it very, very much," said Bilozertchev. "I knew the struggle would be great, but I was ready for it."

both feet on a little springboard and then push off the long horse with their hands, thus acquiring one final boost of aerial energy before they fly into some convoluted somersault.

Men approach the apparatus lengthwise, women go over its middle, and both sexes receive scores based on the predetermined difficulty rating of the vault they choose.

To have hopes of scoring a 10, vaulters must get high above the apparatus, perform their tricks perfectly, then soar far beyond the end of the horse and land the dismount with nary a step, wobble or hop.

Shoushounova will sometimes start a vault not by running and jumping on the board but with a roundoff, which causes her to hit the board backward and with

additional power. From there she does a back handspring to the horse and then pushes off into a straight-body back flip with a 360-degree twist added for good measure. It's almost as hard to describe as it is to do.

If floor exercise contributes moves to the other events, men's parallel bars takes something from all of them.

On these stationary bars, you may see double leg circles — ordinarily the stock and trade of the pommel horse — as well as front flips and handstands from floor-ex, L-supports from rings, a giant swing from high bar and some daredevilish dismounts reminiscent of the vault.

Part of the reason this event gives a gymnast so many options is that it offers him more physical security than any other

event. The bars (11½ feet long and 17-19 inches apart) provide any number of places to hold on and they are also flexible, enabling gymnasts to soar above the apparatus and perform mid-air somersaults.

The closest thing to a circus high-wire act that the world of sport has to offer, the men's high bar competition and the women's uneven bars are more visually exciting than even floor exercise.

And the reason is simple — release moves, mid-air somersaults, startling changes of direction and spectacular dismounts from twelve to fourteen feet in the air.

Bilozertchev, who still lacks feeling in parts of his leg as a result of his car accident, has such great upper-body strength that he does almost everything with one arm. Bilozertchev and his teammates do so many release moves they seem to spend more time in the air than on the bar.

As determined by their finish at the '87 World Championships, a dozen teams will compete on both the men's and women's side in Seoul.

Both the men's and the women's competitions will break down into three separate-yet-interrelated categories: the two-part team competition, consisting of compulsory and optional routines; the all-around, which pits the top thirty-six gymnasts from the team competition (but no more than three from each country) against each other; and the individual event finals, which are sort of like dessert. Following all the tension of the team and all-around competitions, the event finals showcase the top eight specialists on each apparatus (no more than two per country) as determined by their scores during the team competition. Thus, from the first time gymnasts step on the floor, they are scoring points which will have a direct bearing on team, all-around and individual event medals.

Each of those twelve teams will put six gymnasts on the floor, but the lowest score in each event will be thrown out so that only five scores will count. The best a gymnast can achieve is a 10, so the best total a team can post on a single event is 50, which, of course, never happens. Since the men compete in six events and the women in four, the highest

Oksana Omelianchik of the Soviet Union performing on the uneven bars at the Moscow Goodwill Games. With its extraordinary somersaults and rapid spins, the uneven bars is the most dramatic of the women's events.

a team can score during the compulsory round and again during the optional round is 300 (men) or 200 (women). A team's compulsory and optional scores are added together to determine the team championship.

When you compare the progress of one gymnast to another, treat one-tenth of a point as you would one run in baseball. Thus, if one gymnast trails another by three-tenths with four of the six events completed in the men's competition,

Second to Dimitri Bilozertchev in the all-around at the 1987 World Championships, Yuri Korolev of the U.S.S.R will challenge his teammate for the gold at Seoul.

that's comparable to a 3-0 lead with six innings of a baseball game completed. Relatively comfortable, but scarcely insurmountable. When comparing one team to another, keep in mind that a five-tenths swing on one apparatus is a huge one. And remember, in the all-around and the individual event finals, medals are usually decided by hundredths, not tenths, of a point.

To appreciate how that happens, you need to know how a gymnast loses points with the judges, aside from having the wrong-color flag. Here are some general guidelines.

For landings on vault and floor-ex, or on dismounts from any apparatus which aren't completely tight, deduct one-tenth for each step or hop.

For touching hands to the floor, without support, to regain balance on any landing or dismount, deduct three-tenths.

For falling on vault or off any apparatus, or using the hands to prevent what other-wise would be a fall, deduct five-tenths.

To anticipate where those deductions might come into play, be aware that all ten events have distinct personalities with a separate set of risks and possibilities.

Medals are often won and lost on pom-mel horse and balance beam because they're the easiest to fall off. Nobody falls off the rings or parallel bars, while all the men will intentionally fly off the high bar and then try to grab hold again. The uneven bars showcase the most intricate dismounts, beam the most breath-taking mounts. Watch floor-ex carefully because it is a test of a gymnast's general tumbling skills, which translate directly to the vault.

Regardless of who steps forward to win medals in Seoul, the pleasure in watching gymnastics competition at the Olympic level is that you can't fail to be both entranced and thrilled by some of the most beautiful, intricate and difficult-to-achieve movements in the world of sport. ∎

SHOOTING

by Tony Imbimbo

● *Men*
Free rifle
Air rifle
English match rifle
Free pistol
Rapid-fire pistol
Running game target
Air pistol

● *Women*
Standard rifle
Air rifle
Sport pistol
Air pistol

● *Open*
Skeet
Trap

To U.S. skeet shooter Matthew Dryke, clay pigeons are sitting ducks even though they travel up to 120 miles an hour and are only four and a half inches in diameter. Dryke, the 1984 Olympic Champion, can gun down 200 of them in 200 shots.

Tony Imbimbo is a freelance writer who contributes to *Sports Illustrated*, *Runner's World*, *High School Sports* and other national magazines.

But with an Olympic gold medal on the line and TV cameras watching, even the sharpest of shooters get edgy. At this level of competition, one nervous twitch can cost a gold medal.

Perfection under pressure is what makes shooting one of the most competitive sports in the Olympic Games. Since 1896, no one has won more than two individual gold medals, and only eight people have done that. For Dryke to become the United States' next two-time gold medalist it will take as much will as skill, because this year's Olympic competition promises to be more pressure-packed than ever.

In past Olympic Games, competitors completed their required rounds, and whoever had the highest score won the gold. This year, with the introduction of a new "finals" round, the four, six or eight best shooters of each event will meet head-to-head in a shootout. Points scored

in the final are added to a shooter's previous score. If that results in a tie, the shooter with the highest score in the final wins. In ten of the events, if a winner still doesn't emerge, shooters fire one shot at a time until all but one person has missed. That person gets the gold. In the other three—running game target, rapid-fire pistol and sport pistol—another final round is held to determine the winner.

"It's such a mental game," says Launi Meili, a U.S. World Cup champ and one of the top contenders in the women's air rifle and standard rifle events. "It puts you under a lot more pressure because each shot is timed. If the wind

Matthew Dryke of the U.S. rarely misses, especially when shooting clay pigeons with a .12 gauge shotgun. He will be seeking his second consecutive Olympic gold at Seoul.

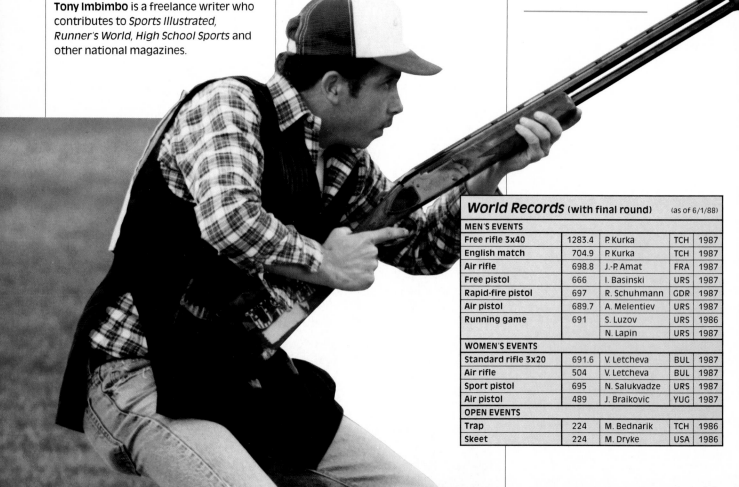

World Records (with final round)				(as of 6/1/88)
MEN'S EVENTS				
Free rifle 3x40	1283.4	P. Kurka	TCH	1987
English match	704.9	P. Kurka	TCH	1987
Air rifle	698.8	J.-P. Amat	FRA	1987
Free pistol	666	I. Basinski	URS	1987
Rapid-fire pistol	697	R. Schuhmann	GDR	1987
Air pistol	689.7	A. Melentiev	URS	1987
Running game	691	S. Luzov	URS	1986
		N. Lapin	URS	1987
WOMEN'S EVENTS				
Standard rifle 3x20	691.6	V. Letcheva	BUL	1987
Air rifle	504	V. Letcheva	BUL	1987
Sport pistol	695	N. Salukvadze	URS	1987
Air pistol	489	J. Braikovic	YUG	1987
OPEN EVENTS				
Trap	224	M. Bednarik	TCH	1986
Skeet	224	M. Dryke	USA	1986

The women's air rifle competition at Seoul is likely to come down to a duel between Launi Meili of the U.S. (left) and Vessela Letcheva of Bulgaria (right). Letcheva narrowly edged Meili in the 1987 World Cup.

comes out, you don't have a chance to wait it out; you've just got to take your best shot."

Meili speaks from experience. At the 1987 World Cup in Suhl, East Germany, this 24-year-old set a world record in the air rifle competition, scoring 396 points out of a possible 400. Yet in the finals round, she placed second to Bulgaria's top gun, Vessela Letcheva, and had to settle for a silver medal.

"It's fair because everyone has to shoot under the same conditions," Meili says. "It's just something you have to develop and train for. And hopefully it will create more interest for the fans."

The competition is broken down into thirteen events. Seven are men's events, four are women's and two—trap and skeet shooting—are open to both. Shooters use one of three weapons—rifle, pistol or shotgun—to fire at a variety of targets, some of which are moving, some stationary and some visible for only

seconds at a time. With the exception of the clay pigeons in skeet and trap shooting, targets are ten-ring circles, and shooters can score between one and ten points per shot depending on which ring they hit.

The events are as follows:

Running game target: Shooters fire at a target superimposed on a lifesized picture of a wild boar as it crosses a ten-meter-wide opening fifty meters away. In the first round of thirty shots, shooters have five seconds to fire one shot each time the boar crosses the opening. In the second round of thirty shots, the shooter has two and a half seconds to shoot. It is the only event in which shooters can use a scope on their .22 caliber rifles.

English match rifle: From a prone position, shooters fire sixty shots with a .22 caliber rifle at a half-inch bullseye fifty meters away.

Free rifle and standard rifle: The same target and distance as in the English match, but shooters fire from each of three positions—prone, kneeling and standing. Men take forty shots from each position; women take twenty.

Air rifle: Using a .177 caliber air rifle, shooters fire sixty shots (forty in women's event) at a target ten meters away. The bullseye is a one millimeter dot (1/25 of an inch).

Rapid-fire pistol: The program consists of two rounds of thirty shots each, fired in six strings of five shots. The five oval-shaped targets are twenty-five meters away. In the first two strings, the targets are exposed for eight seconds; in the next two for six; and finally for only four seconds. Shooters must fire one shot at each target in the allotted time.

Free pistol: Shooters fire a .22 caliber pistol at a two-inch bullseye fifty meters away.

Sport pistol: Consists of two rounds of six five-shot series. In the first round, the shooter must complete each series in six minutes, shooting at a two-inch bullseye. In the second round, shooters have three seconds for each shot at a 4 x 6-inch bullseye.

Air pistol: Using a .177 caliber air pistol, shooters fire lead pellets at a target ten meters away. The bullseye is twelve millimeters in diameter (smaller than a dime).

Skeet: Using a .12 gauge shotgun, shooters fire one shot at each of 200 four and a half-inch clay pigeons traveling up to 120 miles an hour. The clay pigeons are released one or two at a time from two houses.

Trap: Two hundred clay pigeons are released one at a time, and shooters have two shots to hit each target, using a .12 gauge shotgun. ■

SWIMMING

by John Powers

● Men	● Women
50 m. freestyle	50 m. freestyle
100 m. freestyle	100 m. freestyle
200 m. freestyle	200 m. freestyle
400 m. freestyle	400 m. freestyle
1500 m. freestyle	800 m. freestyle
100 m. breaststroke	100 m. breaststroke
200 m. breaststroke	200 m. breaststroke
100 m. butterfly	100 m. butterfly
200 m. butterfly	200 m. butterfly
100 m. backstroke	100 m. backstroke
200 m. backstroke	200 m. backstroke
200 m. medley	200 m. medley
400 m. medley	400 m. medley
4 x 100 m. free relay	4 x 100 m. free relay
4 x 200 m. free relay	4 x 100 m. medley relay
4 x 100 m. medley relay	

Not so long ago, the Olympic swimming pool was America's private bathtub. In 1948, U.S. men swept every gold medal. In 1976, the last time everyone in the world showed up, Americans won all but one, which was claimed by a Briton who trained in the States.

"I expect us never again to dominate the way we did at Montreal," says Indiana University coach James "Doc" Counsilman, who coached the U.S. men's team in 1976. "Because we had so much talent that year—and the rest of the world didn't."

At Seoul this summer, American men will be fortunate to win five of sixteen gold medals. Matt Biondi, who could earn seven medals in all, should claim the 100 freestyle, Tom Jager the 50 and Pablo Morales the 100 butterfly, and these three should also help the U.S. to a couple of relay titles.

But the rest of the gold medals will be spread among as many as half a dozen nations, from West Germany to Hungary, Sweden to the Soviet Union. And the U.S. women, who won eight of fourteen golds as recently as 1972, may win only two.

....

John Powers, 1982 Pulitzer Prize winner for national reporting, has covered the Summer Olympics for the *Boston Globe* since 1976. He is the author of *Mary Lou* (1985), the story of American gymnast Mary Lou Retton.

That would represent a dramatic shrinkage from 1984, when the Soviet Bloc was absent and the American men and women claimed twenty of twenty-nine events. "We dominated swimming at Los Angeles," says Don Gambril, who coached the 1984 U.S. team. "But put the East Germans in there and our women finish a distant second. I don't like to think about it, but it's the truth."

The East Germans have ruled women's swimming since 1973, when they turned up in force at the quadrennial World Championships and left everybody in their backwash. And the rest of the world has been catching up to the American men, who posted 1987's world-best times in only three of sixteen Olympic events.

"Without a doubt, the world has caught up with the U.S. in men's swimming," says Texas coach Richard Quick, who'll be in charge of the U.S. team in Seoul. "If we scored the meet in a championship fashion, the U.S. would still win because we cover all the events better than anyone else. But the days of dominance may be over for at least a while."

The top man in the individual medleys is now a Hungarian (Tamas Darnyi). The best backstroker is a Russian (Igor Polianski), the supreme distance specialist a West German (Rainer Hankel). "There are great athletes in Europe, same as here," says Gambril. "And their facilities are way ahead of where they were after the war."

Olympic-size (50-meter) pools are no longer a rarity on the Continent, and swimmers and their coaches there have access to the same technical and medical knowledge the Americans always have had. "Swimming coaches here have been very frank about what they're doing," says Gambril. "And we've shared it with everyone else in the world."

The Americans have also shared their scholarships, inviting foreigners to join top college varsities, where they can hone their techniques in modern natatoriums against swimmers who will form the core of the U.S. team.

Italy's Giovanni Minervini, ranked second in the world in the 100 breaststroke last year, swam for UCLA. West Germany's Thomas Fahrner, third in the 200 freestyle, competed for Southern California. New Zealand's Anthony Mosse could be found at Stanford, Sweden's Stefan Persson and Tommy Werner at California, Suriname's Anthony Nesty at Florida, Poland's Wojciech Wyzga at Arizona.

"The two best swimmers on my team are from Spain," says Counsilman, who coached Mark Spitz at Indiana. "They'll take the technique they learned here, they'll end up coaching and their country will improve."

Thus does swimming's gospel spread, and it has been showing up in ranking lists, which now resemble a UN roster. Last year's top man in the 200 freestyle, once an American preserve, was Sweden's Anders Holmertz. France and Switzerland each won silver medals in the sprints at the 1986 World Championships, Denmark a bronze in the 200 butterfly. The East Germans, who never bothered much with the men's side, won the 4x200 relay, which the Americans once took for granted. And the world's most versatile swimmer may be West Germany's Michael Gross, who won two golds and two silvers in Los Angeles.

No global parity exists among the women, though. The East Germans would have swamped everybody had they been at Los Angeles, and they'll make up for it at Seoul, where they could win twelve of fifteen races. They ranked first globally in all but three Olympic events last year, and it was no accident.

No country ever came so far so quickly in any sport as the East Germans did in two years during the early seventies. Their women were all but invisible at Munich in 1972, failing to win a gold medal. Two years later, they were undisputed World Champions. In 1976, they shattered Olympic records in every race they won, usually by stunning margins. Ulrike Tauber lowered her mark in the 400 individual medley by more than 20 seconds. Kornelia Ender, who won four gold medals, took nearly three seconds off the standard in the 100 freestyle.

Mary T. Meagher of the U.S. already appears slightly ahead of her opponents as she launches herself into the water at the start of a race. The world record holder in both the 100 and 200 butterfly, she will be a strong threat for the gold in these two events at Seoul.

The GDR "mädchen" have spent the past dozen years whittling those times even farther. Coming into 1988, Kristin Otto (100 free), Heike Friedrich (200 and 400 free), Anke Mohring (800 free), Cornelia Sirch (200 back), Silke Horner (100 and 200 breast), Birte Weigang (100 butterfly) and Kathleen Nord (200 butterfly) were all ranked first in their events. (In setting the world record in the 800, Mohring broke the standard established last summer by Janet Evans, only to see the 16-year-old American take it back last March.) "And they're backed up tremendously by other girls who are just as good," says Counsilman.

The East Germans use the hothouse method of team development, and they have ideal conditions—a small country with complete state support and first-rate biomechanical and sports medicine laboratories.

"In the Eastern Bloc countries, it's part of the government's propaganda program to do well in the Olympic Games and, probably, to beat the U.S.," says Quick. "So some of their best physiologists and psychologists are involved in the effort. That's their single focus. Everything is directed toward doing well in the Olympic Games."

Unlike the U.S. or the Soviet Union, where members of the national team may live thousands of miles apart, East Germany's swimming hierarchy has no problem supervising and communicating with its key people. "They can pick up the phone and have all of their top coaches in Berlin in three hours," says U.S. Swimming executive director Ray Essick, who'd need a fleet of Learjets to accomplish the same thing at the governing body's headquarters at Colorado Springs.

When the East Germans made their breakthrough, rumors circulated among their rivals that they were using wonder drugs or tampering with gender. "At least we look like women," sniffed U.S. freestyler Shirley Babashoff in 1976.

The truth was that the East Germans were both fast and feminine. They just had better training methods—whatever they were.

Unquestionably, the East Germans found ways to use science to their benefit earlier than anybody else did. In a sport which is timed to the hundredth of a second, minute changes in stroke mechanics, diet, conditioning and psychology can make major differences in performance.

Matt Biondi

Not since Mark Spitz rolled a seven at Munich in 1972 has an Olympic athlete won that many medals at one Games. But Matt Biondi could match that feat at Seoul, though unlike Spitz' achievement they probably won't all be gold.

Biondi, who graduated from the University of California-Berkeley last year, was an unknown in 1984 when he made the U.S. team as a relay member and won a gold. But he won seven medals at the last World Championships—three golds (100 free, 400 free and the medley relay), a silver (100 butterfly) and three bronzes (50 and 200 free and 800 free relay). Nobody—male or female—earned more, and nobody seems likely to at Seoul, either.

Biondi plays water polo in his spare time, which has dwindled so much that he's hired a Washington agent to screen interview requests. Spitz didn't have to do that until *after* the Games.

Swimming has come light years from the Twenties, when an American would win a fistful of unchallenged medals and go off and make Tarzan movies. Johnny Weissmuller's winning time in the men's 100 freestyle in 1928 (58.6) wouldn't even have gotten him a medal in the women's race in 1976. The U.S. 800 freestyle relay team that Don Schollander anchored in 1964 would have finished three-quarters of a lap behind the American quartet four years ago. And Spitz's winning times in the 100 and 200 freestyles in 1972 don't even rank among the top 25 U.S. marks now. The top man in the world in the 100 free last year—Biondi—swam a 49.34, nearly two seconds faster than Spitz's time at Munich.

Swimming's standards are simple and absolute—if you aren't getting faster, you're getting slower. Yet the days when swimmers could chop a couple seconds from a global mark are waning.

"World records are getting tougher to break now," says Gambril. "They aren't falling like they used to. You'll see some world records broken at Seoul, but you won't see 20 of them."

Kristin Otto

East Germany's Kristin Otto is not only faster than everybody else, she is more durable as well. At 16, she won three gold medals in the 1982 World Championships. At 20, she earned six medals—four gold (100 free, 200 individual medley, 400 free and medley relay) and two silver (50 free and 100 butterfly) and set a world record in the 100 free.

Otto, who lives in Leipzig, would have been the poster girl of the 1984 Olympics had the GDR not boycotted. But she was still young enough to continue for another quadrennium and injuries (a pinched neck nerve ruined her 1985 season) haven't stopped her.

No woman in the world has ranked among the top ten in as many events for as many years as has Otto. Now, she goes to Seoul as the centerpiece of the GDR women's team, which should win more Olympic medals than all its rivals combined.

World Records (as of 6/1/88)								
EVENT		**MEN**				**WOMEN**		
Freestyle	50m	22.18	P. Williams	SAF	1988	24.98	Yang Wenji	CHN	1988
	100m	48.74	M. Biondi	USA	1986	54.73ʳ	K. Otto	GDR	1986
	200m	1:47.44*	M. Gross	FRG	1984	1:57.55	H. Friedrich	GDR	1986
	400m	3:47.38	A. Wojdat	POL	1988	4:05.45	J. Evans	USA	1987
	800m					8:17.12	J. Evans	USA	1988
	1500m	14:54.76	V. Salnikov	URS	1983				
Backstroke	100m	55.14	I. Polianski	URS	1988	1:00.59ʳ	I. Kleber	GDR	1984
	200m	1:58.14	I. Polianski	URS	1985	2:08.60	B. Mitchell	USA	1986
Breaststroke	100m	1:01.65*	S. Lundquist	USA	1984	1:07.91	S. Hoerner	GDR	1987
	200m	2:13.34*	V. Davis	CAN	1984	2:27.27	A. Higson	CAN	1988
Butterfly	100m	52.84	P. Morales	USA	1986	57.93	M. Meagher	USA	1981
	200m	1:56.24	M. Gross	FRG	1986	2:05.96	M. Meagher	USA	1981
Medley	200m	2:00.56	T. Darnyi	HUN	1987	2:11.73	U. Geweniger	GDR	1981
	400m	4:15.42	T. Darnyi	HUN	1987	4:36.10	P. Schneider	GDR	1982
Freestyle relay	4x100m	3:17.08	McCadam, Heath, Wallace, Biondi	USA	1985	3:40.57	Otto, Stellmach, Schulze, Friedrich	GDR	1986
	4x200m	7:13.10	Sitt, Henkel, Fahrner, Gross	FRG	1987				
Medley relay	4x100m	3:38.28	Carey, Morales Moffet, Biondi	USA	1985	4:03.69	Hoerner, Gressler Kleber, Friedrich	GDR	1984

*World record set at Olympics.   r=performance in first leg of relay.

Swimmers now train hundreds of hours to shave tenths of a second from a record, and their workouts are more demanding than Weissmuller ever imagined. The Mission Bay Makos, one of the nation's top clubs, churn through 10,000 yards a day (20,000 for distance specialists), and spend an extra hour in the weight room.

"There've been times during really hard sets when I'll stop and ask myself, 'What am I doing this for?'" said Mike O'Brien, who won the 1500 freestyle at Los Angeles. "I constantly have to remind myself."

Practices are inescapably monotonous, as swimmers log lap after lap, clinging to kickboards or wearing dragsuits. To get through them, top swimmers create mind diversions while they stare at the bottom of the pool.

"You have to play games with yourself," said Tracy Caulkins, who won three gold medals in 1984. "You have to imagine yourself swimming against the best people in the world."

The only reward for the daily drudgery is faster times. If they don't come, depression and soul-searching usually follow.

A year before he won three gold medals in 1984, U.S. sprinter Rowdy Gaines went through a grim summer when he seemed to be dead in the water. His low point came at the Pan American Games in Caracas, when he finished third behind a Venezuelan.

More recently, some Olympians have been taking time off between Games to rest and recharge. Both of the U.S. gold medal winners at the 1986 women's World Championships — Betsy Mitchell and Mary T. Meagher — skipped last summer's big meets to catch their breath and clear their heads.

Meagher — a.k.a. Madame Butterfly — had been ranked first in the world in the 200 fly for eight years and won it by a mile (along with the 100 fly) at Los Angeles. The prospect of another chlorinated season with nobody in pursuit struck her as unproductive.

Mitchell, the world record holder in the 200 back, took three months off after the 1987 winter season, swam the outdoor nationals mostly for fun and called it a season. Those two are rarities, though. Most world-level swimmers feel constant pressure from below and are always looking for an edge.

Janet Evans

She didn't even qualify for the U.S. team at the last World Championships, but 17-year-old Janet Evans will be the brightest new face on the American women's squad at Seoul. She's half a head shorter (5'4½") than her East German rivals and barely heavy enough (99 pounds) to make a splash, but Evans set three world records (400, 800 and 1500 freestyles) last year and won three events at the U.S. championships.

Evans, who lives in Placentia, California and swims for Fullerton Aquatics Sports Team (FAST), gets up at 5 a.m. and regularly puts in 6500 meters before school begins, with another 8000 after school and before homework. It's this determination that makes her a threat to win three medals at Seoul, and her duel with East Germany's Anke Mohring over 800 meters should be one of the best of the Games.

West Germany's Michael Gross will undoubtedly be dueling America's Matt Biondi in the 200 freestyle at Seoul. World record holder in the 200 butterfly, which he is seen swimming here in the 1985 European Championships, Gross is one of the most diversely talented swimmers in the Games.

Some fiddle endlessly with stroke technique, looking for more efficient ways to propel themselves through the water. U.S. Swimming, the national governing body, just built a flume in Colorado Springs where athletes swim in place while water rushes by and videotape whirs. Some sports scientists and coaches think the flume can provide valuable data about swimming mechanics. Others aren't so sure.

"There are so many variables," says Counsilman. "Research can clarify many things, but it's not going to cause many breakthroughs. It just confuses a lot of people."

Counsilman actually created one of swimming's most profound breakthroughs in 1970 when he began applying Bernoulli's principle to swimming. "You don't really pull the hand straight back," he said. "You use a sculling motion and the lift principle. You use lateral movement. Even so, it took fifteen years for that to be really accepted."

Swimmers also experiment with starting techniques. Some use a jackknife start, diving deep off the blocks. Others use a "track" start, crouching like runners, then flinging themselves forward. And backstroker David Berkoff goes with a submarine start, where he swims the first 20 meters underwater before popping up.

Swimmers still shave their bodies — some even shave their skulls — before big meets to reduce friction. Some wear skinsuits so thin they look like body paint. Two races in the 1984 Games — the men's 800 relay and the women's 100 backstroke — were decided by less than a tenth of a second. And the women's 100 freestyle was a dead heat, with Americans Carrie Steinseifer and Nancy Hogshead hitting the plate in 55.92. Maybe if one had shaved closer....

"A guy called me today about a new material he had for caps and suits," Gambril chuckled last winter. "He said it's as near to the dolphin's skin as you can get." ■

WRESTLING

by Herm Weiskopf

●*Men*

Freestyle and Greco-Roman
48 kg. (106 lbs.)
52 kg. (114.5 lbs.)
57 kg. (125.5 lbs.)
62 kg. (136.5 lbs.)
68 kg. (149.5 lbs.)
74 kg. (163 lbs.)
82 kg. (181 lbs.)
90 kg. (198.5 lbs.)
100 kg. (220 lbs.)
100 to 130 kg. (220 to 286 lbs.)

Jacob's all-night wrestling bout with an angel in Genesis 32 may well have been the ultimate "match made in heaven." Right behind it, though, could be the showdown between Soviet and American freestyle grapplers in Seoul. There the U.S. will have a realistic chance to end the dominance of its arch rival, which has won every freestyle team title in the Olympics and Worlds since 1961.

America's hopes are not as lofty in Greco-Roman, in which no holds are permitted below the hips. The U.S.S.R. and Bulgaria are virtual locks for first and second. But the U.S. just might break up the Romania-Poland-Hungary phalanx in the tussle for the next three spots.

American progress in both styles is largely the result of having solved the dispute as to which official body controls amateur wrestling in the United States. With the ascendency of USA Wrestling, the American wrestling program has finally emerged from the confusing power struggles of several years ago.

Herm Weiskopf, a staff writer at *Sports Illustrated* for more than thirty years, has written nine books on various sports topics.

Andre Metzger (top) must defeat Nate Carr in U.S. Olympic Trials if he is to have the opportunity to dethrone Arsen Fadzayev of the U.S.S.R. (bottom) as the world's finest 68 kg. freestyle wrestler.

In an effort to make wrestling more appealing to the public, FILA, the sport's international governing body, introduced several new rules after the 1980 Olympics.

Matches were reduced from three to two periods of three minutes each, with a one-minute break between them. The shortened bout requires both wrestlers to attack and counterattack continually or be penalized for stalling. And for the first time in Olympic competition, ties will be resolved not by complicated scoring criteria, but by the first man to score in an overtime period.

Most exciting of all, in both styles, is the new five-point throw, which raises by a point the maximum score for a single maneuver. The five-pointer begins with both men down on the mat and requires that the aggressor hoist his foe until his hips are above the lifter's head. And then with proper balance and timing he throws his opponent to the mat and onto his back. You can expect to see several of these breathtaking moves in the Olympic Greco-Roman bouts, though they are less common in freestyle.

A good-mark scoring system decides who advances to the next round in each of the ten weight classes. The more decisively a wrestler wins, the more points he earns, up to a tops of four for a pin, default, disqualification or superior decision (when one wrestler builds up a lead of fifteen points in his match).

In international bouts a pin is recorded when a wrestler's shoulder blades are forced even momentarily to the mat.

During bouts, one man wears a blue singlet, the other a red one. When points are scored, the referee raises the appropriate number of fingers. You can tell

who has been awarded the points by which hand is put up, for the referee wears a blue band on the right arm, a red one on the left. One point is given for a takedown (bringing a man from his feet down to the mat) and for a reversal (switching from being controlled by a foe to being in control of him). Throws earn from two to five points.

Wrestlers must be prepared to make offensive thrusts while also being defensively on guard. Since matches were reduced to a pair of three-minute periods, the Americans, who are among the best-conditioned of athletes, have used their training to advantage. Watch how U.S. freestylers try to pressure and wear down opponents, and how they shoot for leg takedowns more often than most others. The Soviets have blast-off explosiveness and use combinations by executing feints and then slamming in at a vulnerable spot.

Although no team medals are awarded, team scores are nevertheless compiled, with points awarded in inverse order for the top ten finishers: one for placing tenth, ten for being first.

American freestyle coach Jim Humphrey includes lots of potential high scorers on his squad, particularly John Smith, the 1987 World Champion at 62 kilograms. In addition, Mark Schultz is a three-time World Champion and 1984 gold medalist

at 82 kilograms, and at 74 kilograms the U.S. boasts two of the world's best: 1984 Olympic gold medalist Dave Schultz, Mark's brother, and Kenny Monday, the only non-Soviet winner and the Outstanding Wrestler at this year's Tbilisi Cup, a tournament in the Soviet Union which many consider to be the toughest in the world. Unfortunately, each team is entitled to only one entry per weight.

The U.S.-U.S.S.R. scrap could hinge on the 68 and 130 kg. classes. At 68 kg., Andre Metzger, a silver and bronze medalist at the last two World Championships, and Nate Carr, the 1986 World Cup champ who has dropped from 74 kg., will battle to make the U.S. team. At Seoul, either would be favored if not for Arsen Fadzayev of the U.S.S.R. who has not lost internationally since 1983. Bruce Baumgartner, the 1984 Olympic champion, in 1986 became the first U.S. 100-130 kg. World Champion. He, too, would be a solid choice were it not for one man — Aslan Khadartsev, a former world titlist at 100 kg. who moved up in 1987 and dethroned Baumgartner.

Soviet emigré Pavel Katsen, who came to the U.S. in 1979, is coach of the Greco-Roman squad — the "Katsenjammer Kids." How high the team places depends greatly on Mike Houck's health. In the 1985 World Championships, the 90-kilogram Houck became the first American to earn a gold medal in Greco-Roman. Alas, a bad back has clouded his future.

"The Europeans' techniques are much better than ours, and they are very aggressive," Katsen says. "But Americans are in better shape and have more willpower. They are brave creatures." They will have to be. ■

EQUESTRIAN

by Ann Martin

●Open
Individual Dressage
Individual show jumping
Individual three-day event
Team dressage
Team show jumping
Team three-day event

S uccess in Olympic equestrian events requires highly skilled riders and trainers and, equally important, horses of exceptional quality. Despite several vast European breeding projects, it

....

Ann Martin, lives in London and covers major international competitions for the *London Evening Standard*, the *Birmingham Post* and *Horse and Hound and Field*.

remains extremely difficult to find horses capable of jumping the necessary heights and distances and able to master the complicated movements of dressage. Those performing at Seoul will be extraordinary.

In addition to the marvelous horses you will see, Seoul will also feature a host of contestants not previously eligible for the Games. Following the 1984 Games, the Féderation Equestre Internationale, which governs the sport, ruled that professionals could apply for reinstatement

Joe Fargis of the U.S. on Touch of Class wins the 1984 Olympic gold medal in show jumping. In this event, "the horse is 80 percent of the partnership," says Britain's David Broome, a former show jumping World Champion.

to a "competitor-amateur" status, enabling them to take part in Olympic competition. Large numbers of them did, and as a result the field at Seoul will be representative of the world's best.

Olympic equestrian competition includes three separate disciplines: dressage, show jumping and the three-day event. It is also one of the few sports where men and women compete against each other on an equal basis.

Dressage is the most aesthetic of the three, in which superb riders in elegantly-

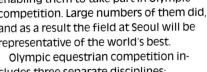

cut clothes guide their mounts through a series of intricate movements.

Each test lasts ten minutes and includes the halt and various forms of the walk, trot and canter, and the spectacular and difficult pirouette, the passage and piaffe. Few horses like executing the latter, which is a collected, elevated, cadenced trot on the spot.

Movements are judged on a scale of 1 to 10 in which the horse's performance, the rider's position and the method of control are evaluated.

It would constitute a major surprise if the team and individual gold did not come to Europe. Germany's Ann-Kathrine Linsenhoff and Switzerland's Christine Stückelberger are serious contenders.

The three-day event is the most thrilling challenge at the horse trials, a grueling test of all-around ability, boldness and courage.

The first day's competition is a seven and a half-minute dressage of varied movements, included to judge the horse's calmness, suppleness and obedience.

The second day consists of a speed and endurance test, broken into four sections of about four and one-half miles each: a warmup road test, a steeplechase, another road test, and a cross country run requiring contestants to jump over thirty fences. The course designer, former British Olympian Hugh Thomas, has set the trial on unusually hilly terrain, thereby placing a high premium on a horse's stamina and fitness.

The final day's show jumping is set over a twisting course of moderately high obstacles to test whether the horse has retained its obedience, elasticity and energy after the exhausting cross country phase.

Scores are based on time over the course, and penalties are costly. For the first refusal, for instance, a rider is penalized 20 points; for the second, 40; and for the third refusal at the same obstacle, the rider is disqualified.

Disqualification from any of the three competitions means elimination from the entire event.

Great Britain's Ginny Leng, current World and European Champion, who broke her arm in twenty-three places in a terrible fall in 1977, is seeking to become the first woman ever to win the Olympic three-day event. She will have to beat, among others, Bruce Davidson of the U.S. and New Zealand's Olympic gold medalist, Mark Todd. The U.S., Great Britain and New Zealand should fight for the team medals.

The easiest to follow of the equestrian disciplines, show jumping is also the most spectacular. The course, designed by West German Olaf Petersen, is 700 to 900 meters long with twelve to fifteen fences. Each jump is between 1.4 and 1.6 meters high.

Riders must complete the course twice at a rate no slower than 400 meters per minute or penalties are earned. Penalties are also awarded if fences are knocked down or if the horse refuses a jump. A rider is disqualified if the horse refuses three jumps over the entire course.

In the team competition, four riders participate, though only the best three scores count. The top eight teams in the first round move on to the second.

An important rule change since 1984 has eliminated the requirement that jumpers carry a minimum weight, thus giving the lighter riders an advantage.

The U.S. will attempt to defend its Olympic title against the challenge of its arch rival Great Britain, which earned the silver medal in the 1984 Games and won European Championships in 1985 and 1987. But the Canadians, with the exceptional combination of Ian Millar and Big Ben, and the French, led by the new European champion Pierre Durand on Jappeloup, are also strong contenders, along with the Swiss. ■

ROWING

by Jack Frailey

● **Men**
Single scull
Double scull
Quadruple scull
Coxless pair
Coxless four
Coxed pair
Coxed four
Coxed eight

● **Women**
Single scull
Double scull
Quadruple scull
Coxless pair
Coxed four
Coxed eight

Although it's called rowing on the Olympic program, as the viewer will see it in Seoul it bears little resemblance to what people have experienced in a rowboat. Few viewers will be able to say, "I've done that. I know what's going on out there on the water." Rowboat rowing is done by the upper body and arms alone because the seat doesn't move; Olympic rowing uses the full thrust of the legs as well. A rowboat is so flat-bottomed that it's impossible to tip over; a rowing "shell" (the term for the boat) is basically so unstable and tippy that the rowers must constantly balance it with their bodies and oars—much like high-wire circus acrobats use their balance poles.

Six of the fourteen events at the Games are rowed by scullers, using two oars each, one in each hand; the other eight by rowers using both hands on one oar (sweep). Though the two rowing techniques are basically the same, a single sculler is alone in the smallest boat raced, while eight sweep swingers join in the largest. The "eight" and some of the smaller sweep boats have coxswains in them, too, who steer and frequently "call the signals" according to the coach's

Jack Frailey, board chairman of the U.S. Rowing Association, has written frequently on rowing for newspapers and magazines in the Boston area.

particular race plan. "Blind" boats—those without coxswains—are steered by a rower turning the rudder through a cable and pulley system with his foot.

Tactics are important. The first fifty strokes are particularly crucial; a crew has a poor chance to win if it is more than a half-length behind the leaders at that point. The stroke rating, or racing beat (the number of strokes per minute) is at its highest at the start—sometimes as high as 48-50—and the first difficult decision in the race is how long a start to take.

After the first thirty or forty strokes the crews begin to settle to a rating they will sustain with little change until the finishing sprint. For most crews this rating will be 33-38 strokes per minute.

Subsequent tactics include short bursts of ten to twenty strokes at more than "cruising" power (sometimes at midpoints decided by the crew and coach in advance) taken either to maintain one's position within attacking range of the leaders, or, if in the lead, to lengthen it or to respond to such a challenge.

Such periodic testing will continue among the crews, until the decision is made to sprint for the finish line. The timing of that decision has affected the outcome of many races. Medals will be won or lost by tenths, even hundredths of a second—and to begin one's sprint a stroke too late or early can make that difference.

The course is 2000 meters long and will be covered by the men's eight-oared shell in about six minutes and by the women single scullers in about eight, so rowing is more a "distance" sport than is the mile in track. Hence the highest peak of proficiency, coordination and skill is required to propel the shell without wasted effort. Most spectators will find it hard to detect the slight variations in style and technique of these superb crews but will be impressed simply by their seemingly effortless fluidity. This will be most apparent in the eights, which require the absolute zenith of teamwork and coordination.

In the United States, rowing is one of the lesser known of the Olympic sports, but abroad it is very popular indeed. In

New Zealand only rugby draws more athletes, and the dominance of the Eastern Bloc countries causes them to think about it as their "medal sport." Since 1966 the East German men have qualified for all but four of 127 final races, and their women have missed only three of 96. At the last Olympics, however, Romanian women won every event except the eight, in which they silvered behind the U.S.

But American hopes are high, and the men are favored to win the most prestigious event, the eights, for the first time since 1964—off their convincing 1987 World Championship gold last year. The men's coxless four, which won in 1986, and the women's eight, which was a close second in 1987 and won in 1984 in Los Angeles, will also be strong contenders.

These recent successes can be traced mainly to an ever increasing pool of elite sweep rowers, produced by the new

training and coaching methods championed by national technical advisor Kris Korzeniowski.

The centerpiece of the Games will be the fourth, and probably last, Olympic meeting of the two titans, Pertti Karppinen of Finland and Peter-Michael Kolbe of West Germany, who have been constantly at each other since 1976 when Karppinen beat Kolbe to win the first of his three consecutive gold medals in the single scull. Though narrowly beaten by Kolbe at the World Championships in 1986 and again in 1987, Karppinen knows a victory at Seoul would mean a fourth

Finland's Pertti Karppinen hopes to become the first rower in history to win a gold medal in four Olympics.

consecutive gold. No one else has won more than three golds in the history of Olympic rowing. In addition to worrying about each other, they have to worry a lot about Thomas Lange of East Germany, who beat them both at the 1987 World Championships. This could be the race of the century. ∎

The power and intensity which drive the fragile shells are evident in the women's single scull event at the 1985 World Championships.

SOCCER

by John Powers

● *Men's event*

The sport is played and watched by more people than any other on earth. It is known as football by everyone except Americans, who call it soccer. And even though the Olympic tournament is nowhere near as important as the quadrennial World Cup, soccer is still the most popular event in the Games and has been for the last three Olympiads.

In 1976, nearly 60,000 spectators sat in the rain at Montreal to watch the East Germans beat the Poles. In 1980, with their team not even in the final, more than 100,000 Muscovites jammed Lenin Stadium. And in 1984, an even larger crowd watched France defeat Brazil in the Rose Bowl. More than a fifth (1.4 million) of all spectators at the Los Angeles Games paid to see soccer, even though the host U.S. team did not advance beyond the first round.

Olympic soccer may not have the impact of the World Cup, which features all of the planet's top players. But it is played by the same nations, according to the same rules, with much the same style and tactics.

Only sixteen countries will make it to Seoul from a qualifying pool of 112, which was whittled down by two years of regional elimination tournaments. They will be split into four groups for round-robin play, with the top two in each advancing to the quarterfinals and the final two playing for the gold medal.

"It's like World Cup," says Lothar Osiander, a San Francisco waiter who coaches the U.S. team on a per-diem basis. "You just try not to lose because a couple of ties gets you into the next round. So the pace is a little slow, since you are trying not to give goals away. But in the quarterfinals, you have to win."

Usually the victors are East European nations, who have captured every Olympics since 1952 (except for 1984, when they boycotted) by using teams filled with state-supported amateurs.

After non-socialist nations complained that they were at a permanent disadvantage, FIFA (Fédération Internationale de Football Association), which runs the sport worldwide, ended its ban on professionals before the 1984 Games. Now, only players from Europe and South America who have competed in the World Cup are ineligible.

Here seen playing against Italy (in white) in the Los Angeles Games, for which it qualified by virtue of being the host country, the U.S. is not yet strong enough for real world class competition. The three victories in a regional tournament, which made the team eligible for Seoul, however, marked an important step forward in the U.S. soccer program.

Even that will change four years from now in Barcelona, when everybody under the age of twenty-three will be admitted, as FIFA tries to protect the uniqueness of the World Cup by making a clear-cut distinction between its centerpiece event and the Olympics.

"That will be better for us," says Osiander. "Most of our players are college seniors who are under twenty-two. All we have to do is keep them together for another year."

The Americans have always been at a disadvantage at the Olympic level. They no longer have a professional outdoor league from which to draw, and their national teams are usually put together from whatever material is at hand.

"If we have all our players, we can compete with the rest of the nations in North and Central America and the Caribbean," says Osiander. "For us, the problem is availability. During college season, I don't have college players. During indoor season, I can't have indoor players. And when the indoor players are available, I have to re-school them for the outdoor game."

The United States still qualified for Seoul by being one of two teams to advance from its regional tournament.

But they have no illusions about making the awards stand. The Eastern Bloc, which swept all three medals in 1972, 1976 and 1980, will be back in force. And now that professionals are allowed, countries like Brazil, Yugoslavia and Italy are using the Games as a tuneup for the 1990 World Cup.

So while Olympic spectators won't see legendary players like Argentina's Diego Maradona, Belgium's Jean-Marie Pfaff and Brazil's Socrates, they will see world-class soccer, played in familiar fashion. The faces may vary, but the styles are the same.

"South Americans play much more of a skill game," says Osiander. "They're very much involved with the ball. Europeans are more physical and tactical, with emphasis on running."

The Americans, who must blend collegians with indoor professionals who are often naturalized citizens, don't have the luxury of an established style. "We're not strong enough to say we'll play our own game," says Osiander. "We look at our opponents and decide how we can disrupt their play."

Their moment may come in Barcelona, where the rules finally favor their kind of player. "For us, just getting to the Olympics is a success," Osiander says. "Whatever happens after that is just gravy, a bonus." ■

WATER POLO

by Mark Muckenfuss

● *Men's Event*

The pass hasn't even reached you and already your defender is on your back, one hand in the air, the other — underwater and out of sight of the referee — latched onto your suit, pushing your hips down.

You grab the ball and kick furiously, trying to stay above water, but it's no use, your head slips beneath the surface. Still you hold onto the ball.

Hooking your man with your free elbow and driving your legs with all of your strength, you manage to turn toward the goal. Relying on your instincts, you raise your arm above the churning waters and shoot at a goal you cannot see. But the ball goes low, allowing the goalie to block it. Your defender breaks for the counterattack by pushing off against your side. He's already a body-length ahead as you struggle to the surface, gasping for breath, and try to catch him before he reaches the other end of the pool.

Welcome to the hole, or two-meter position, the centerpost of water polo where all is fair when a player has his hand on the ball, and even when he doesn't, as long as it happens beneath the surface of the water and out of sight of the referees.

Water polo has been a part of the Olympics since 1900, making it, along with soccer, the oldest team sport still played in the Games. It combines the skills of swimming, the strategic elements of soccer and basketball and the strength of football. The basic idea of the game, played in seven-minute quarters, is for the six fieldmen on each team to try to shoot the ball past the goalie and into the opponent's goal at the other end of a 20 x 30-meter pool which is 1.8 meters (5'11") deep. Teams must shoot within 35 seconds or lose the ball, and players cannot

Mark Muckenfuss is a Los Angeles-based writer. He covers water polo and swimming for *Swimming World* magazine and is the editor of *Swimming Technique*.

grasp the ball with two hands, take it underwater, or push off the bottom of the pool.

Offensive play centers around the hole man. He "sets" in front of the goal, two meters out, with the other players fanned out in a semicircle four to eight meters away from the goal. The hole man is relied upon either to shoot the ball or draw a foul. The latter is easy, since his defender is committed to doing everything in his power to keep him from shooting.

Fouls are a critical part of the game. For ordinary fouls, the offended player must either pass the ball off or put it back in play and retain possession of it himself. He cannot, however, shoot the ball until another player has touched it. So by fouling the hole man, the defender eliminates the man closest to the goal as a scoring threat.

A player has three seconds to put the ball into play from the time a foul is called. This is called the dead-time. Any infraction incurred during this time results in a 35-second ejection of the offending player.

Most water polo goals are scored while a team has a man advantage. Typically in this situation the team in control of the ball will line a man up in front of each post of the goal, while the remaining four set up on the outer perimeter, working the ball back and forth, looking for a good shot.

In addition to major fouls such as kicking, punching, holding and showing disrespect to an official, which require a 35-second ejection, the four-meter penalty is probably the most significant in the game. Called when a player within four meters of the goal is blatantly fouled.

Action in the bronze medal game at the 1986 World Championships, in which the U.S.S.R. edged the U.S.A. (in blue) 8-6 in four overtimes.

Manuel Estiarte turns a good Spanish team into a potential medalist by his presence. He led all scorers in the 1986 World Championships with 28 points.

in order to prevent an impending shot on the goal, it results in a free shot from the four-meter mark, similar to a penalty kick in soccer. It is unusual to see more than one or two penalty shots in a game, but they can be critical as top international games are often decided by a single goal.

Competition among the best national teams has continued to get tighter and tighter in recent years. A decade ago there were two or three teams capable of battling for a gold medal. In Seoul, there will be five legitimate contenders, making this one of the best Olympics ever for water polo.

Traditionally, East European teams have dominated, and Yugoslavia and the U.S.S.R. have to be considered the favorites again. West Germany, the United States and Italy are also serious threats for the top medal. Spain is a dark horse, but could figure in the medal winnings.

Playing styles vary among these six teams. The Soviets tend to play a more disciplined, "set-up" offense. Although they possess a potent counterattack, they tend to be the most static of the teams offensively. On the other end of the spectrum is Spain. Lacking a strong hole man, the Spaniards rely on quickness, constant movement and the deadly arm of Manuel Estiarte, arguably the best water polo player in the world. The Italians also favor a more mobile style of offense, while West Germany and Yugoslavia fall somewhere in the middle. The U.S., led by hole man Terry Schroeder, who was a member of the 1984 silver medal-winning squad, is the best fast-breaking team.

In the past ten years either the Yugoslavs or the Soviets have won nearly every major international tournament. The games between these rivals should prove to be the most exciting. On the other hand, the Western teams would love to break up the East European Olympic control, which goes back to 1960, the last time a Western nation (Italy) won the gold. ∎

BOXING

by Liam Nolan

● Men

Light-flyweight — 48 kg. (105.5 lbs.)

Flyweight — 51 kg. (112 lbs.)

Bantamweight — 54 kg. (119 lbs.)

Featherweight — 57 kg. (125.5 lbs.)

Lightweight — 60 kg. (132 lbs.)

Light-welterweight — 63.5 kg. (139.5 lbs.)

Welterweight — 67 kg. (147.5 lbs.)

Light-middleweight — 71 kg. (156.5 lbs.)

Middleweight — 75 kg. (165 lbs.)

Light-heavyweight — 81 kg. (178.5 lbs.)

Heavyweight — 91 kg. (200.5 lbs.)

Super-heavyweight — 91-plus kg. (Over 200.5 lbs.)

The smallest men in the Olympic boxing competition are the battlers in the light-flyweight division, weighing no more than 48 kilograms. The biggest are the super-heavyweights, weighing more than 91 kg. To be able to move from the short, sharp and spiky to the big, powerful and destructive constitutes, for the spectator, one of the great attractions of Olympic boxing.

Most of the boxing you see on your television screen is of the professional variety — men fighting for money. And that word "fighting" is advisedly chosen, even though purists will still stick to the strict use of the term "boxing."

Professional fighting differs from what you will see during the Olympic tournament in a number of ways. To begin with, while professional bouts range from four to fifteen rounds, Olympic boxing matches are limited to three rounds, each of three minutes duration with a one-minute interval between them. And whereas professionals do not wear a shirt, an amateur must wear a shirt and headguard. Olympic boxers in the six classes from 48 to 63.5 kg. wear eight-ounce gloves, which is what all professional fighters wear, while boxers in the six heavier classes wear ten-ounce gloves. The gloves are white on the knuckles, to help the judges identify correctly-

....

Liam Nolan, formerly the sports editor of the *Sunday Journal* in Dublin and BBC-TV boxing commentator, is currently director general of Ireland's National Olympic Committee.

delivered punches. It is also worth noting that in Olympic competition a knockdown is of no more value than any other scoring punch.

More significantly, professional boxers tend to want to finish their business in

the ring as quickly as possible, caring little for tradition, nice appearance, or an emphasis on style at the expense of power. "Get to him, hit him hard, hurt him, knock him out," could well serve as the professional's credo.

Such a credo was initially quite alien to the brand of amateur boxing which evolved in Britain. Often referred to today as the "British style" in recognition both of its place of origin and the fact that it was the method the British used, it was based on the tactics of a straight left lead, delivered with the right foot forward and the right hand held high to protect the head.

The boxer worked from an upright stance, and the straight left was used as a jab to the face, keeping the opponent off-balance, flustered and perhaps annoyed. It was, and is, a good point-scoring punch. If used intelligently, it can also serve as a measuring blow for a right cross, and it still attracts many practitioners.

In time, however, the influence of professional boxing spread to the amateur ranks, altering the purity of the British style. Hooks and upper-cuts and the wrong-way-around fighters coming out of a crouch and leading with the right hand eventually affected the amateur style. Americans took up the professional tactics and flowered. Then the Cubans followed suit and became even more adept, dominating Olympic competition.

Throughout all of these new developments, however, the Eastern Bloc countries stuck to the traditional style, studying correct punch delivery, movement, defense, the technique of scoring points. At Seoul you will see these skills still at work with their boxers, as well as with the British, who, although they occasionally unearth a natural hooker, more often than not display the same skills they have always employed.

One of the most important stories of the Olympic boxing tournament is the announced boycott by Cuba. The Cubans are arrogant, supremely fit, exciting — and talented. They won seven of twelve weight classes and finished second in two others in the 1986 World Championships and took ten of eleven finals at the 1987 Pan American Games. Led by two-time light-heavyweight World Champion Pablo Romero and middleweight Angel Espinosa, the outstanding boxer at the '87 Pan Ams, Cuba was favored to win as many as seven golds in Seoul.

Without the Cubans, the tournament will be wide open.

The South Koreans in particular expect to take advantage of the Cuban boycott. They see themselves on the verge of becoming a new world boxing power. Based on their performance at the Asian Games in Seoul last year, where they won twelve of twelve finals, they may be right. They have a chance to win two or three gold medals at Seoul, with 1987 World Cup flyweight champion Kim Kwang Sun, light-flyweight Oh Kwang-Soo and light-welterweight Kim Ki-Taek all strong contenders.

Korean boxing progress stems partly from increased attention to diet and weight training and partly from more time spent preparing the athletes. With their immense physical strength, Koreans have the capacity to absorb fierce punishment and still deliver massive blows which lack finesse but have a powerful sleep-inducing effect.

United States' hopes to recapture the boxing prestige it has lost in recent years to Cuba will depend heavily on fighters like featherweight Kelcie Banks, here seen battling Marcos Cristofalo of Argentina in the 1987 Pan Am Games.

Welterweight Ken Gould of the U.S. in the 1987 Pan Am Games, where he captured the silver medal. Gould won the gold at the 1986 World Championships, and with the absence of the Cubans has to be considered the favorite at Seoul.

And the fact that these are the first Summer Olympics to be held in Asia since the Tokyo Games in 1964 will undoubtedly provide a stimulus for all Asian athletes to perform at the top of their abilities.

However powerful their motivation, the Asians will still have to contend with perennially strong European boxers, especially those from East Germany and the U.S.S.R. Outstanding prospects for Olympic medals include: Ulli Kaden of East Germany, who won the super-heavy-weight title at the 1987 European Championships; his teammate, Henry Maske, who dominated the middleweight division at the same championships; 20-year-old Andreas Tews, also of East Germany, who won the flyweight final at last year's European Championships against the experienced Hungarian Janos Varadi, and Soviet light-middleweight Vasili Shishov.

Romanian welterweight Francisc Vastag and heavyweight Arnold Vanderlijde, the 1984 Olympic bronze medalist from the Netherlands, could also be tough to beat. And although the Americans need to pull themselves together after the beatings administered in recent years by the Cubans, I think they will feature strongly at Seoul, turning up some of the most exciting ringmen in the Games. Watch especially for Kelcie Banks, who took the featherweight gold at the 1987 Pan American Games, flyweight Arthur Johnson, a four-time U.S. champion, and welterweight Ken Gould, a defending World Champion.

Olympic boxing matches are presided over by a referee, whose only job it is to control the bout, and five judges who determine the winner. Each judge must award twenty points in each round to the boxer he thinks won the round. If the judge sees it as even, he assigns twenty

to each fighter. A closely contested round would typically be scored 20-19. At the end of the bout, each judge must designate a winner. If on his scorecard the points are even, the judge will then make a choice based on his evaluation of which fighter was the most aggressive.

What do the judges look for? Most important, of course, is the quantity—and quality—of the successful punches. To score points, blows must be delivered directly with the knuckle part of the closed glove on any part of the front or sides of the head or body above the belt. Blows landing on the arms don't count.

The quality of the "infighting"—the exchanges which occur when the boxers come together, shoulder to shoulder and trade punches—is also important.

There are some competitors who specialize in this aspect of the sport, who will be willing to absorb some blows in order to get to close quarters where they will then exercise their skill and strength to land body shots and uppercuts.

You have to watch carefully to see whether the blows are actually landing, or are being blocked by arms or fists. The judges will be looking to see who, in their view, gets the better of each such rally, and they will reward him accordingly.

The judges also watch for the boxers' defensive skills, their abilities to duck inside the arc of a punch and make it miss; the capacity to "catch" a punch on the glove like a baseball player using the mitt; the clever use of footwork to dance backward or sideways or both ways, out of range; the eye-hand coordination that allows an incoming shot to be deflected by the forearm. Technically, these skills do not score points, but they can make the difference in a close bout.

It must be noted, however, that though there are uniform scoring rules, not all the judges from the different countries interpret them uniformly.

Eastern Europeans, for example, lay great emphasis on such technical skills as evading punches by parrying, slipping and ducking, and also by intelligent footwork, clever counter-punching, maneuvering an opponent so that he is trapped in a corner or on the ropes.

They sometimes claim that American judges are more impressed by flashy aggression from all-action boxers who throw more "professional-looking" hooks than straight punches, and who are adept at putting together clusters of punches known as combinations.

There are a number of practices which are prohibited, such as hitting on the back, hitting an opponent who is down or in the act of getting up, hitting below the belt, butting with the head, thrusting with the elbow, hitting or flicking with the open glove, pulling the opponent into the punch, holding and hitting, and persistent ducking below the belt.

In amateur boxing, a referee may caution a man for an infringement of the rules. A caution doesn't mean a mandatory loss of points, and it is usually delivered by the referee stopping the action and indicating that a boxer should, for example, keep his punches up or watch the careless use of his head. But if the referee stops the bout, takes the arm of the boxer and indicates to all five judges individually that he is issuing a warning, then expect that boxer to have points deducted from his score. It could even lead to his eventual disqualification.

If past Olympics are any indication, one thing is certain: boxing at Seoul will present a dazzling array of superbly coordinated athletes, fit, strong, swift and clear-headed, going about their business with a range of mesmerizing and ever-varying abilities. They will be a pleasure to watch. ∎

The dominance of Cuban boxing is symbolized by already legendary super-heavyweight Teofilo Stevenson, who won three Olympic gold medals from 1972 to 1980. Here he is seen in the 1986 World Championships on his way to winning the gold.

DIVING

by Russ Ewald

● *Men*
Platform
Springboard

● *Women*
Platform
Springboard

Whether in the pike, as seen here, or in any of the other standard positions, Greg Louganis of the U.S. tends to do everything better than all other divers. At Seoul he will try to become the first male diver to win Olympic gold medals a second time in both the platform and springboard events.

Rarely does an athlete succeed in dominating a sport as completely as Greg Louganis of the U.S. has come to dominate diving. The premier diver in the world today, and arguably the best of all time, Louganis, in the 1984 Olympic Games, became the first male diver in fifty-six years to win the gold in both the springboard and platform events. And the real diving drama at Seoul focuses on Louganis' efforts, at age 28, to be the first male diver in the Olympics ever to win both a second time. (Only Pat McCormick of the U.S. has managed this feat before, winning the 1952 and 1956 women's competition.)

Louganis' accomplishments speak to his extraordinary gifts. Through last spring he had won forty-four national titles, sixteen more than any other diver. He is the only diver to receive on two occasions a perfect score of 10 from all seven judges for a dive (both times an inward 1½ somersault in pike position on platform). He has achieved the highest scores in history in both the springboard (755.49 points for eleven dives) and platform (717.41 for ten dives).

When Louganis first broke the 700-point barrier to win the platform event at the 1984 Olympics, U.S. co-coach Ron O'Brien remarked, "It's like someone going 30 feet in the long jump or running the 100 meters in 9.5 seconds."

Louganis' ability to excel off each of the widely-varying boards — the springboard is only three meters high and very flexible, the platform ten meters and solid — is a result of an ideal (5'9", 160 pounds) build for diving, his unusual strength and agility and an abundance of natural talent. His strength allows him to leap off the springboard higher than opponents, giving him more time to execute his dives, and his agility permits him to spin and twist quickly during the few seconds prior to entering the water. His background as a professional dancer

Russ Ewald, an associate editor of *Swimming World*, has covered diving for the magazine since 1984.

Gao Min of the People's Republic of China is one of the superb young divers the Chinese will bring to Seoul. The 1986 women's springboard World Champion, she holds the record for the highest score ever compiled by a woman (582.90) in a ten-dive springboard event.

has also helped, enabling him to transfer some of the grace and artistry of the dance to his aerial acrobatics off the board.

Louganis has been able to remain in the sport because of a new liberalized interpretation regarding amateur eligibility. After the 1984 Olympics, U.S. Diving, Inc., the sport's national governing body, ruled that divers could earn money through endorsements and appearances as long as they either use it for expenses or put it in a trust fund. Previously, it was rare for American divers to stay in the sport after college graduation, but five of the seven members of the 1984 Olympic team are still competing at ages ranging from 23 to 28. Besides Louganis and Bruce Kimball, the 1984 silver medalist on platform, there's Kelly McCormick, silver medalist on women's springboard and daughter of Pat; Michele Mitchell, silver medalist on women's platform; and Wendy Wyland, bronze medalist on women's platform. Megan Neyer, the 1982 springboard World Champion, is another top American veteran.

In past Olympic competition, the U.S. has dominated, winning 115 out of 200 medals and 43 of 66 golds. At the 1984 Games, in an unprecedented feat, all seven Americans won medals.

Even though the U.S. has been able to retain almost all of its top divers, it may not be as successful in this Olympics

Michele Mitchell, U.S. silver medalist on platform in the 1984 Games, will have to be in her best competitive form if she is to challenge the Chinese women at Seoul.

because of the improvement of the other teams, especially the People's Republic of China. In 1986 the U.S. was outmedaled for the first time ever at a World Championships when China took two golds, all four silvers and one bronze.

China's strength is no accident. China's coaches recruit potential divers at an early age, selecting them through a precise set of physical criteria. They look for girls no taller than 5'3½" and boys 5'6" or less with flat backs, hyperextended elbows, thin legs and a high degree of flexibility.

This emphasis is paying dividends, especially in the women's competition where the Chinese have developed such champions as Gao Min, 18, the world's leading springboard diver the past two years; and 17-year-olds Chen Lin and Xu Yanmei, the top platform performers internationally in 1986 and 1987 respectively. Gao Min has the highest score ever (582.90) for a women's ten-dive springboard event.

China relies on its veterans in men's competition, led by Tan Liangde, 23, the silver medalist on springboard in both the 1984 Olympics and the 1986 World Championships; Tong Hui, 25, last year's World Cup platform champion; and 29-year-old Li Kongzheng, the Olympic platform bronze medalist who has been studying and training at the University of Texas the last four years.

Another team to watch is the Soviet Union, which revitalized its declining women's program with an influx of talented youngsters, including phe-

nomenal Elena Miroshina. As a tiny (4'8", 70 pounds) 13-year-old last year, Miroshina set a world scoring mark (508.65) on women's platform (eight dives) and won the European Championships.

Women's springboard looks to be the most competitive diving event of the Seoul Games with strong challenges to the Chinese coming from Soviet standouts Marina Babkova and Irina Lashko; Brita Baldus of East Germany; and Daphne Jongejans of Holland, who has turned down modeling offers to dive at the University of Miami (Florida).

Diving has progressed dramatically since it was added to the Olympics in 1904. In the early days there were only fourteen platform and twenty springboard dives. The list approved by the international technical committee now includes 71 platform dives and 66 on springboard. The difficulty of dives has increased to the point where a double somersault from the platform, considered dangerous in the early 1900s, has yielded to the performance of the reverse 3½ somersault today.

A dive is scored by taking the awards of the seven judges—which range from 10 for a perfect performance to zero for a failed one—and eliminating the highest and lowest to prevent partiality. The remaining five scores are totaled and multiplied by three-fifths. The resulting number is then multiplied by the degree of difficulty which is assigned to each

dive, ranging from 1.3 for a simple inward tuck to 3.5 for a 4½ somersault tuck off platform. That formula gives the score of the dive. The highest possible score for the most difficult dive is 105 points.

In evaluating a dive, judges consider the approach, takeoff, height and arc of the dive, and the diver's technique and grace during passage through the air and entry into the water.

During the execution of the dive, the competitor assumes one of four body positions: straight, no bends anywhere; pike, a single bend at the hips with the legs straight at the knees; tuck, the knees together pulled into the body like a cannonball; and free, a combination of the straight and either tuck or pike positions used for twist dives. Judges reward dives which exhibit tightness of the tuck, compactness of the pike, straight legs, pointed toes and feet together.

When entering the water, the body must be straight and vertical. The best entry is when the diver punches through the water with no splash. It's called a "rip entry" because it sounds like a sheet tearing.

Not all judges emphasize the same things: International judges tend to reward overall difficulty more highly than do American officials, who are impressed by smooth entries.

Divers must overcome an enormous amount of emotional pressure as they stand around for minutes at a time, waiting for their chance to spend a few seconds in the air. The pressure is compounded by the fact that there are no second chances; one bad dive can eliminate a competitor from the medal quest.

Diving competitions are also not without their strategic maneuvers. The first half of each event is the required dives. Each diver must perform one dive from each of five categories (forward, back, reverse, inward and twisting) on springboard and four of the five on platform. In addition, men must perform a handstand dive from platform. The total degree of difficulty for the five springboard dives must not exceed 9.5, and the four platform dives 7.6.

The concluding portion of the program, however — the "optionals" — is in part a mental game in which divers try to gain a psychological advantage over their opponents. This cannot be better illustrated than in the classic platform rivalry between Louganis and Kimball. Louganis uses an exceptionally difficult list of dives to put pressure on from the start and saves his toughest for last in order to catch up if he gets behind. Kimball, who has beaten Louganis six times in national meets, though not since 1984, goes with a very conservative list, depending on superb execution accented by rip entries and performing his toughest dives early to rattle his opponents.

However subtle the tactical moves, to see these superb athletes spinning rapidly like gyroscopes after exploding high off the three-meter springboard or somersaulting down at speeds up to 33 miles per hour from the ten-meter platform is to appreciate what marvelous physical skills they possess. ∎

Li Kongzheng displays the grace off the platform that brought him the bronze medal in the '84 Games. He finished second to Louganis in the 1986 World Championships.

FIELD HOCKEY

by Patrick Rowley

● *Men's event*

● *Women's event*

You mean to say they play hockey on grass? Well, not exactly. It started out that way when the modern version of the game was formulated in London in the 1860s, but today almost all top international field hockey is played on artificial surfaces.

To many—especially Americans—field hockey is thought of as primarily an activity for adolescent girls. But in fact, it is a fiercely competitive game which in the last two decades has shed its low profile and grown into an international sport played in more than one hundred countries. The men and women who compete at continental championships are gifted athletes with a broad range of skills.

The game has affinities with ice hockey and soccer. It is played for two thirty-five minute halves by teams of eleven players on a 100 x 60-yard field.

The object is to hit the 3½-inch hard-plastic ball into the opponents' goal using a hardwood stick. To accomplish this, speedy attacks, crisp passing and tightly disciplined offensive patterns are employed.

To prevent this from happening, a well-padded goalie patrols the goal behind the backs, midfielders and forwards who constitute the team. Only the goalies are permitted to use their hands, feet or other parts of the body to stop the ball.

The field hockey stick is slightly smaller than that for ice hockey, though only the flat side can be used. Players are not allowed to use any part of their bodies or sticks to prevent opponents from hitting the ball.

Patrick Rowley, founder and editor of *World Hockey*, the official publication of the International Hockey Federation, is a British author, journalist and TV commentator.

Great Britain's brilliant goalie, Ian Taylor, makes the surprising 1984 Olympic bronze medalist team a serious threat at Seoul.

Goals are scored in one of three ways: in field play, at penalty corners or from penalty strokes. Field goals are easily the most exciting. It should be remembered, however, that goals can be scored only when the ball is hit from within the 16-yard (14.63 meters) semicircle in front of the goal.

Penalty corners are awarded for deliberate fouls by the defense outside the circle but within its 25-yard line or for accidental fouls within the circle.

One player hits the ball from the goal line to a teammate kneeling at the edge of the circle, who stops it, permitting another teammate to take a shot. The shot must be low enough to hit the 18-inch (46cm.) high backboard in the goal. A lot of corner shots are disallowed for one infringement or another.

A penalty stroke, taken on a spot seven yards (6.40 meters) in front of the goal by a single attacker against the goalkeeper, is awarded for a deliberate foul by a defender inside the circle or for an unintentional foul that prevented a goal being scored.

For years India ruled men's international field hockey, winning eight Olympic gold medals. Dexterous stick-handling and skillful passing techniques mastered on bone-hard surfaces made them hard to beat. But the rest of the world has been catching up fast, the process accelerated by the introduction of artificial surfaces which provide players who previously slogged away on muddy grounds the perfect conditions to perfect their skills.

The Australian men, who won the 1986 World Cup in London, are seeded No. 1. Their outstanding player is Richard Charlesworth, a member of Parliament. In the World Cup final, Australia defeated England (which in the Olympics plays as Great Britain).

With an accomplished goalkeeper in Ian Taylor, Great Britain was the surprise squad at the Los Angeles Olympics, coming in only as replacements for the boycotting U.S.S.R. and walking away with the bronze medal. It has maintained a top ranking and is expected to be a strong contender at Seoul. Pakistan, the 1984 Olympic gold medalist, and India slumped to all-time lows at the 1986 World Cup where they finished in the last two places (11th and 12th). But the Pakistanis, unlike the Indians, have shown every sign of being real challengers again by Olympic time.

There are twelve selected countries in the men's Olympic competition, seeded into two groups of six with the top two in each pool advancing to the semifinals. There will be eight rivals in the women's competition, two more than at Los Angeles. They will play initially in two groups of four.

Teams receive two points for a win and one for a draw. If points are equal at the end of the pool matches, the team with the bigger goal difference (goals for minus goals against) ranks the higher. If the goal difference is equal, the team that has scored the most goals gets preference.

The leading contenders for the men's medals are likely to be Australia, Great Britain, Pakistan and West Germany, with the Netherlands and newcomer South Korea the teams to watch. The Korean men and women have improved dramatically in the last few years.

The Netherlands has dominated women's hockey since World Championships were introduced in 1975. Only West Germany has denied them a clean sweep of titles. The Dutch hold the Olympic, World Cup and European Cup titles and must be favorites again, though Australia has become a serious challenger. ∎

Member of Parliament
Richard Charlesworth relies
on his athletic skills, not his
political wiles, in leading the
Australian field hockey team.

MODERN PENTATHLON

by Steve Lowery

● *Men*
Individual
Team

The first point about the modern pentathlon is that it's not all that modern. Any sport that includes horseback riding and swordplay is not exactly knocking down the 21st-century's door.

Eager to generate goodwill among military men throughout the world, Olympic founder Baron Pierre de Coubertin designed it to celebrate skills presumably needed by an army courier at the end of the 18th century. Translated into a five-day Olympic sport, those skills include the following:

Day 1: A 600-meter ride on an unfamiliar horse over fifteen obstacles.

Day 2: An épée fencing tournament, which can last up to twelve hours. Each fencer faces all others in three-minute bouts. The first touch determines the winner of each.

Day 3: A 300-meter freestyle swim.

Day 4: Shooting with a .22 caliber pistol at a revolving target 25 meters away. Each competitor shoots four rounds of five shots each.

Day 5: A 4000-meter cross country run, the sport's most dramatic component. Starts are staggered according to a competitor's point position after the first four events. The first to cross the finish line, therefore, wins the modern pentathlon.

The modern pentathlon made its first Olympic appearance during the 1912 Games in Stockholm, and since that time a number of adherents have defended its combination of pure athleticism (swimming and running) and precision skill events (riding, shooting, fencing) as the greatest trial of the total athlete. Bill Hanson, executive director of the U.S. Modern Pentathlon Association, argues that it demands more of an athlete

....

Steve Lowery has been a staff writer with *The Los Angeles Times* Orange County bureau since 1984. He has covered a variety of sports from harness racing to professional baseball.

than do the ten different track and field events which make up the better-known decathlon.

"The fact that the modern pentathlon has five fewer events makes a good performance in each that much more critical," he says. "And the fact that the events are far more varied in their approach and execution, I think, makes for the greater test."

The importance of performing well in each event has been proven time and again.

At the 1912 Games, a U.S. Army Lieutenant named George Patton would have finished second based on his performance in four events. But in the shooting competition, which was then the first event, Patton, reputed to be an excellent marksman, refused to use the standard service revolver preferred by the other contestants, choosing instead his own pearlhandled one. He placed twenty-first in shooting in the field of thirty-two, finishing fifth overall.

At the 1968 Mexico City Games, West Germany's Hans-Jürgen Todt saw his hopes of a medal disappear when the horse assigned to him balked three times at an obstacle. So enraged was Todt that after the ride he attacked the horse and had to be pulled away from the animal by teammates.

At the 1984 Los Angeles Games, Sweden's Svante Rasmuson was within forty yards of the finish of the cross country run when he momentarily lost his balance and stumbled. He recovered quickly, but not fast enough to prevent Italy's Daniele Masala from passing him to win the gold. Rasmuson had to be content with the silver.

"One slip, one slightly off day, and you've had it," Hanson said.

Those most likely not to slip in the team event (the combined scores from a

Svante Rasmuson's stumble in the 1984 Games cost him first place, but he still managed to finish with the silver medal.

The last event of the five-day competition, the grueling 4000-meter cross country run determines the winner of the modern pentathlon. Italy's Daniele Masala, looking fresher than he feels on his way to winning the 1984 gold medal, will be a strong contender in Seoul.

nation's three competitors) are the Soviet Union and Hungary. Since the introduction of the team event in 1952, the Soviets have won four team titles and the Hungarians three.

In the individual championships, France's Joel Bouzou, the 1987 World Champion, is a favorite. Others include Hungary's Laszlo Fabian (third in the 1987 World Championships), the Soviet Union's Anatoly Avdeev (fifth), and Masala, the defending Olympic champion. The United States' hopes seem to rest with Rob Stull, the 1987 Pan American Games champion. ■

SCORING

All events except riding are scored against a par of 1000 points. Points are added or subtracted depending on performance.

Riding: A clean ride of less than 1 minute, 43 seconds earns the maximum of 1100 points. Two points are deducted for each second slower. Additional points deducted for falls (60 points), refusals (40) and knock-downs (30).

Fencing: Winning 70 percent of bouts earns 1000 points. Each win over the 70 percent mark is worth an additional seventeen points, and seventeen points are subtracted for each match under 70 percent.

Swimming: Finishing in 3:54 earns 1000 points. Four points added or subtracted for each half-second faster or slower.

Shooting: Each bullet worth up to 10 points (bulls-eye). A score of 194 out of 200 earns 1000 points. Twenty-two points are added or subtracted for each point above or below 194.

Running: Finishing in 14:15 earns 1000 points. Three points added or subtracted for each second faster or slower.

WEIGHTLIFTING

by Doug Cooney

● *Men*

Flyweight — 52 kg. (114.5 lbs.)
Bantamweight — 56 kg. (123 lbs.)
Featherweight — 60 kg. (132 lbs.)
Lightweight — 67.5 kg. (148.5 lbs.)
Middleweight — 75 kg. (165 lbs.)
Light-heavyweight — 82.5 kg. (181.5 lbs.)
Middle-heavyweight — 90 kg. (198 lbs.)
100 kg. (220 lbs.)
Heavyweight — 110 kg. (242.5 lbs.)
Super-heavyweight — 110-plus kg. (Over 242.5 lbs.)

Weightlifting is a classic Olympic sport, requiring the strength of a shot putter, the flexibility of a gymnast and the concentration of a shooter. In few sports is the result as definitive and immediate as with the barbell.

There are two individual lifts performed in Olympic weightlifting competition: the snatch and the clean and jerk. In the snatch, the weightlifter brings the barbell from the floor to overhead in one continuous motion. The lifter may squat under the bar as he raises it, but then he must stand, demonstrating control until the head referee signals a successful lift. The snatch, which requires a wide hand spacing to allow for the rotation of the shoulders, is often referred to as "gymnastics with weights." Demanding great strength and proper technique, it is one of the fastest of all sport movements in the Olympic Games.

The clean and jerk is a two stage lift involving tremendous back and leg strength. The first part, called the clean, entails bringing the bar from the floor up to the shoulders (with a closer hand-spacing than in the snatch). The second half (the jerk) is completed by the weightlifter driving the weight directly overhead to arms length. During the jerk the athlete may split his legs, but then he must bring his feet back in line, exhibiting control for the referees.

Doug Cooney, six-time New England weightlifting champion, has been weightlifting commentator for NBC Sports since 1980. He was the press chief for weightlifting at the 1984 Olympic Games in Los Angeles.

Weightlifters compete in both events on a 4 x 4-meter platform. If a contestant steps off this area, his lift is disqualified. Two of three referees must indicate a lift is good in order for it to count. During the actual lifts, the weightlifter must avoid inconsistent movements such as unlocking the arms with the weight overhead, pressing out in the snatch or the jerk or not demonstrating control while the weight is overhead.

Weightlifting competitions are divided into ten categories from 52 to 110-plus kilograms.

Competitors have three attempts for each of the two lifts. The order in which weightlifters perform is determined by the amount of weight requested, with the competitor requesting the lightest weight going first. Weight is added progressively to the bar in an auction-like setting. Lifters must add at least five kilograms between the first and second round and at least 2.5 kilos between the second and third. Strategy is important here as the athlete and coach must select a starting weight which is not only attainable, but which puts the weightlifter in a competitive position.

This scenario provides an opportunity for gamesmanship, in which the athletes try to rattle their opponents by making the first lift as heavy as possible. The danger of this psychological assault, of course, is that a lifter can burden himself with a weight he can't manage, miss his three attempts and lose.

The heaviest snatch lift completed added to the best successful clean and jerk determines each competitor's official total. Should two contestants tie on total weight, the one with the lighter bodyweight is declared the winnner.

While to the inexperienced spectator weightlifting might appear to be a simple and static act in which strong men walk out on a platform and heft huge weights over their heads, it is neither simple nor static.

The weightlifter who performs for a few short minutes in front of judges and audience has in fact been warming up for a considerable time backstage, lifting progressively heavier weights until he reaches about 90 percent of his maximum.

Warming up is important both psychologically and physically. As each weightlifter adds weight, he is attempting to get a feel for the weight. Sometimes a weight might not feel heavy, but rather "out of the groove." At this point a coach must help with necessary technical adjustments. For example, a comment from the coach like, "You are using your back more than your legs in the pull," might result in the appropriate correction.

When a competitor is crisp and on target, even the heaviest weights can feel light. "I could have lifted another twenty pounds," says a lifter on a good day. In truth, a well-trained weightlifter who has his rhythm makes even maximum weights appear rather easy.

Weightlifting is a sport in which psychological strength is as important as sheer physical ability. Weightlifters not only must be strong, they must have an extraordinary capacity to concentrate as well.

Antonio Krastev of Bulgaria exhibits the intense concentration and determination of the great weightlifters as he competes in the 1985 World Championships. In 1987, Krastev set the world record in the super-heavyweight class with a snatch of 216 kgs.

World Records (as of 6/1/88)

EVENT		SNATCH				CLEAN & JERK				TOTAL		
52kg.	117.5kg.	He Zhuoqiang	CHN	1987	153kg.	He Zhuoqiang	CHN	1987	265kg.	He Zhuoqiang	CHN	1987
56kg.	123.5kg.	He Yingqiang	CHN	1987	171kg.	N. Terziiski	BUL	1987	300kg.	N. Shalamanov*	BUL	1984
60kg.	148kg.	N. Shalamanov*	BUL	1986	188kg.	N. Shalamanov*	BUL	1986	335kg.	N. Shalamanov*	BUL	1986
67.5kg.	158.5kg.	I. Militosian	URS	1988	200.5kg.	M. Petrov	BUL	1987	352.5kg.	A. Behm	GDR	1984
75kg.	168.5kg.	B. Gidikov	BUL	1986	215kg.	A. Varbanov	BUL	1986	377.5kg.	Z. Stoichkov	BUL	1984
82.5kg.	183kg.	A. Zlatev	BUL	1986	225kg.	A. Zlatev	BUL	1986	405kg.	Y. Vardanian	URS	1984
90kg.	195.5kg.	B. Blagoev	BUL	1983	233.5kg.	A. Khrapaty	URS	1987	422.5kg.	V. Solodov	URS	1984
100kg.	200.5kg.	N. Vlad	ROM	1986	241.5kg.	P. Kuznietsov	URS	1984	440kg.	Y. Zakharevich	URS	1983
110kg.	203kg.	Y. Zakharevich	URS	1987	248kg.	Y. Zakharevich	URS	1986	447.5kg.	Y. Zakharevich	URS	1986
+110kg.	216kg.	A. Krastev	BUL	1987	265.5kg.	L. Taranenko	URS	1987	472.5kg.	A. Kurlovich	URS	1987

*Now called Naim Suleymanoglu (TUR)

Bulgarian Asen Zlatev, 1987
bronze medalist at the World
Championships, in the
process of a successful snatch
lift. Notice the wide hand
spacing necessary for the
snatch as opposed to the
clean and jerk.

Standing over the bar, the lifter puts everything out of his mind, imagining only the feel of a successful attempt. Weightlifters say it is something like seeing a motion picture and then trying to re-experience it. This is why, during the actual competition, contestants rarely watch each other for fear that observing a failed attempt might negatively affect their own chances.

Above all, champion weightlifters must be confident. Coaches and competitors alike stress that the difference between a gold and silver medal is frequently more a question of confidence than inherent athletic ability. The great weightlifters know, in spite of the pressures of international competition, that they are going to win. Those who have this supreme confidence are said to possess "the iron will."

The techniques of weightlifting require endless practice to master. In the snatch lift, watch the way the weightlifter keeps the bar close to his body and moves quickly under it. The initial pull off the floor starts slowly until the bar passes the knees. As the bar passes the waist the lifter will actually pull himself under the barbell while it still has upward momentum. He tries to hit the bottom position just as the weight reaches its maximum height. At this point the athlete secures his balance and stands, demonstrating control. The snatch lift requires perfect technique. A slight miscalculation and the weight will miss the "groove" either in front or behind. This is an event which requires not only strength but delicate timing and balance.

In the clean, the weightlifter also pulls himself under the bar as it passes his waist. At this point he will rotate his elbows under the bar so that it rests on his shoulders. He then stands immediately, capitalizing on his momentum. Failure to do so can result in a bungled effort—in weightlifting parlance, "buried in the clean." Once upright with the bar on his shoulders, the lifter attempts the jerk portion. While strong arms help, the primary work is done by the legs. Should the weightlifter not drive the bar to arms-length swiftly, the lift will be lost. A well-trained weightlifter utilizes a quick, snappy motion, putting the weight overhead in a fraction of a second.

Most weightlifters lift approximately 100 pounds more in the clean and jerk than in the snatch.

Since the 1960s Eastern Europe has dominated the sport, in particular Bulgaria and the Soviet Union. In Seoul, Bulgaria is expected to excel primarily in the lighter weight classes, with the Soviet team having the edge in the heavier categories. China, which won four gold medals in Los Angeles at the 1984 Olympics, has a chance for at least one gold medal in Seoul, as does Hungary.

The United States, which has not had a men's World Champion since 1969 when Bob Bednarski and Joe Dube won top honors, is unlikely to win a single medal in Seoul. Tommy Kono, eight-time World Champion who has won two Olympic gold medals for the U.S., explains, "Interest in the United States is more with team sports such as football and basketball. The lack of recognition and few rewards result in fewer athletes taking up weightlifting. Athletes tend to gravitate toward sports which generate financial rewards."

In addition to its thorough recruitment of young athletes, Bulgaria owes a great deal of its success to its coach, Ivan Abadjiev, who combines radical training methods with extraordinary motivation to create outstanding world-class lifters.

Foremost among them are Stefan Topurov at 60 kg., who became the first in his class to lift triple body weight in the clean and jerk; Mikhail Petrov, three-time World Champion at 67.5 kg.; and Borislav Gidikov and Aleksandr Varbanov, who will undoubtedly duel for the gold at 75 kg. unless Varbanov decides to move up a class.

In the heavier classes, where the Soviets are strongest, watch for Anatoli Khrapaty at 90 kg.; World Champion Pavel Kuznietsov at 100 kg.; and perhaps the most dominating competitor in the 110 kg. class, Yuri Zakharevich, who dislocated his elbow attempting a world record in the snatch in 1983 but came back two years later to become World Champion.

The battle for the gold medal in the super-heavyweight category should be

Naim Suleymanoglu, representing Turkey in the 60 kg. class, is the only Olympic weightlifter to compete for two countries under two different names. Before defecting to Turkey in 1986, the two-time World Champion lifted for Bulgaria under the name of Sulaimanov.

the best of any Olympics in recent memory, with Soviets Aleksandr Kurlovich and Leonid Taranenko and Bulgaria's Antonio Krastev the leading contenders. Kurlovich, World Champion in 1987, appears the overall favorite based on his tremendous strength and confidence. Taranenko, 1980 Olympic gold medalist in the 110-kg. category, has gained both weight and strength but is said to leave his best lifts in the gym. He does not appear to possess Kurlovich's competitive spirit.

Challenging the supremacy of the Bulgarians and Soviets will be, among others, China's He Zhuoqiang at 52 kg., who attributes his strength to a daily drink of fresh ginseng, royal jelly and ground antler, and, in the 60 kg. class, Naim Suleymanoglu. Considered by many the best weightlifter in the world pound for pound, the two-time World Champion for Bulgaria defected to Turkey during the 1986 World Cup and is expected to represent Turkey in the Seoul Games. ■

YACHTING

by Robert N. Bavier Jr.

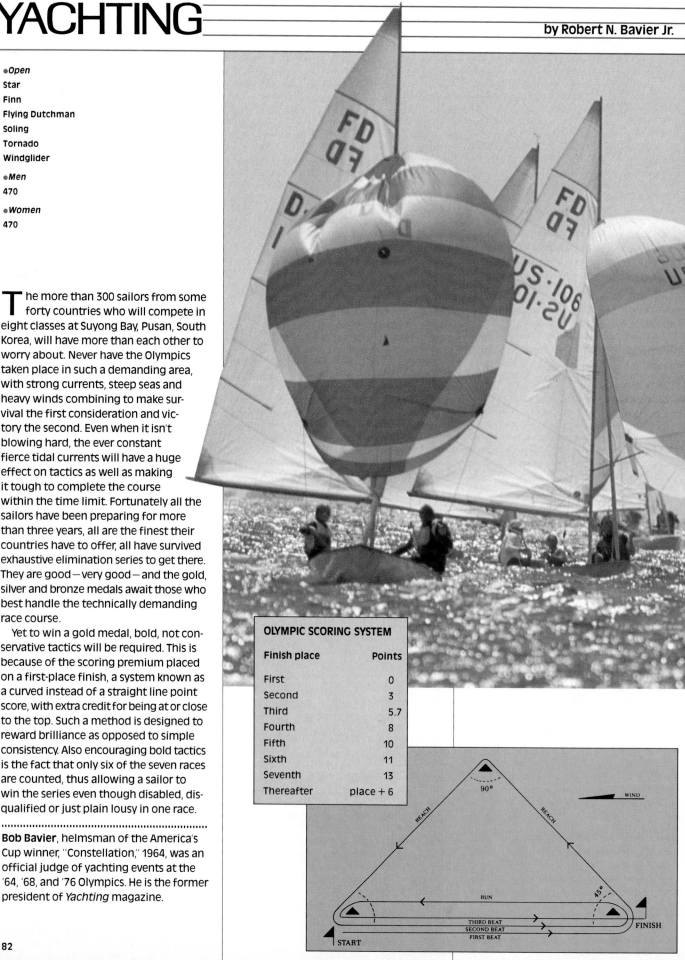

The more than 300 sailors from some forty countries who will compete in eight classes at Suyong Bay, Pusan, South Korea, will have more than each other to worry about. Never have the Olympics taken place in such a demanding area, with strong currents, steep seas and heavy winds combining to make survival the first consideration and victory the second. Even when it isn't blowing hard, the ever constant fierce tidal currents will have a huge effect on tactics as well as making it tough to complete the course within the time limit. Fortunately all the sailors have been preparing for more than three years, all are the finest their countries have to offer, all have survived exhaustive elimination series to get there. They are good — very good — and the gold, silver and bronze medals await those who best handle the technically demanding race course.

Yet to win a gold medal, bold, not conservative tactics will be required. This is because of the scoring premium placed on a first-place finish, a system known as a curved instead of a straight line point score, with extra credit for being at or close to the top. Such a method is designed to reward brilliance as opposed to simple consistency. Also encouraging bold tactics is the fact that only six of the seven races are counted, thus allowing a sailor to win the series even though disabled, disqualified or just plain lousy in one race.

....

Bob Bavier, helmsman of the America's Cup winner, "Constellation," 1964, was an official judge of yachting events at the '64, '68, and '76 Olympics. He is the former president of *Yachting* magazine.

OLYMPIC SCORING SYSTEM

Finish place	Points
First	0
Second	3
Third	5.7
Fourth	8
Fifth	10
Sixth	11
Seventh	13
Thereafter	place + 6

a separate women's division. Women can, if they like, still compete in the other classes, but few will. While women can sail successfully against men, a man's greater strength does seem to provide a slight edge even in such a cerebral sport as sailing.

Who are the strongest contenders? Don't expect a repeat of the U.S. team's remarkable 1984 feat of winning three gold and four silver medals. The Korean waters are rather different from the "home field" advantage which sailing off the California coast gave the U.S. the last time. But do expect the U.S. to do very well, probably better than any other country. Andy Kostanecki, the hardworking (and unpaid) head of the U.S. Olympic Yachting Committee, rates us particularly strong in the Soling, Star and Finn classes, with good medal possibilities in the Tornado, Flying Dutchman and women's 470, and our longest shot in the sailboard and men's 470s.

But who knows? Even in our supposedly weak classes a sharp young American sailor could burst on the scene. Conversely, we could lose out in traditionally strong classes such as the Star. Few of the 1984 medalists will be back, not because they are over the hill (yachting is a sport of athletic longevity), but because few want to repeat a three-year all-out effort just in hopes of making the team. A sentimental favorite who has been there before is Paul Elvstrom of Denmark, who won gold medals in 1948, 1952, 1956 and 1960 and is now competing in the Tornado class with his daughter, Trine, as crew.

The top possibilities for medals, aside from the U.S., include: Soviet Union—Finn and Flying Dutchman; Great Britain—470 men, 470 women and Finn; East Germany—Soling; Denmark—Flying Dutchman, Finn and Soling; France—470 women and Windglider; Sweden—Soling and Star; Switzerland—470 men; Holland—Tornado; Italy—Star; Israel—Flying Dutchman. All that is certain, however, is the fact that the winners at Pusan will have beaten not only the world's best but the elements of Suyong Bay as well. ∎

The billowing spinnakers of the Flying Dutchman class add beauty and color off the coast of California in the 1984 Games. The treacherous winds off the Korean coast will test the skill and courage of those unfurling the majestic sails in Suyong Bay.

Some of the risks you will undoubtedly see crews take in these circumstances will involve chancing a capsize or breakdown by carrying a spinnaker in a difficult wind or splitting from the fleet in hopes of moving from third to first place, despite the possibility of thereby dropping to tenth or lower.

The classes which will race at Pusan are as follows: the Soling, a 27' keel boat with a crew of three; another keel boat, the 22'8" Star, with a two-person crew; the 20' Tornado catamaran (also two); and three centerboarders (retractable keel), the first two of which—the 19'10" Flying Dutchman and the 15'5" 470—have two-person crews. The 14'9" Finn and the Windglider, essentially a sail-propelled surf board, are both singlehanders. In the 470 class, there is for the first time

BASKETBALL

by Larry Eldridge

● *Men's event*

● *Women's event*

The world has waited sixteen years for another dream rematch in men's basketball between the United States and the Soviet Union. In Seoul, it could finally happen.

The Americans will field their usual young, quick, explosive team featuring a combination of great shooters, high-leaping rebounders and all-around skilled performers. Coach John Thompson, whose highly successful career at George-town includes one national championship and two runner-up finishes, will choose his squad from the finest collegians available, players like Charles Smith of Pitt, J.R. Reid of North Carolina, Danny Manning of Kansas, David Rivers of Notre Dame, Rex Chapman of Kentucky — and David Robinson, a 1987 graduate of the U.S. Naval Academy. Whoever finally makes the team, it has to be favored to win the gold medal.

Meanwhile the Soviets — also as usual — are expected to be the principal challeng-ers. They'll have their standard collection of big, strong, rugged types who special-ize in controlling the boards, setting up good percentage shots, slowing down the pace. and making the other team play their game. And of course they'll also have their usual advantages of considerable international experience plus the team cohesiveness gained from playing toge-ther for several years.

This lack of experience playing together as a team has hardly been insurmounta-ble for the United States in the past, and it isn't expected to be this time, either.

As for the game itself, international rules and those used in the U.S. college game have moved closer in recent years,

Larry Eldridge, sports editor for *The Christian Science Monitor* since 1975, has covered college, professional and inter-national basketball for nearly thirty years. His work has appeared in Dutton's annual *Best Sports Stories*, *Reader's Digest* and *Sporting News*.

so there's not as much of a problem for American players — or TV viewers — as there once was. Both games are played in 20-minute halves, and the Olympic rule requiring the team with the ball to shoot within 30 seconds parallels the 45-second clock, which has been adopted recently in collegiate basketball. The college game has also just added the three-point basket. The Olympic three-point range, 20'6", is slightly longer than the college's 19'9".

Significant differences remain, however: international rules permit a player to take two steps after receiving a pass on the move instead of the one allowed in the United States; and the dramatic "alley-oop" in American basketball, featuring a player leaping into the air, catching a pass and dunking, is illegal in Olympic competition. Players who catch a pass while airborne must touch the ground before shooting. The international game also tends to be rougher, with each team permitted seven team fouls, as opposed to the six in college basketball, before the bonus rule goes into effect, giving the team which is fouled the choice of two free throws or possession of the ball.

Perhaps the hardest thing the Americans will have to get used to is the fact that an official doesn't have to touch the ball when it changes hands. The team gaining possession just takes the ball out of bounds, passes it in, and goes. The danger is that American teams, used to having an extra second to regroup as the ball is handled by an official, can be caught flat-footed after a turnover as the opposing team just grabs the ball and races downcourt.

But the rule differences are not likely to confuse the Americans for long. Barring the unforeseen, the U.S. and the U.S.S.R. figure to fight it out for the gold medal in the long-awaited rematch of their controversial 1972 final in Munich, which the Soviets won 51-50 on a still hotly disputed last-second basket. But of course there are several other teams who have different ideas — plus enough talent to pull off an upset if anyone gets too cocky or complacent. And all it takes is a brief glimpse at recent history to show that things don't always happen the way they're supposed to in these Olympic basketball tournaments.

In the old days, of course, they did. U.S. teams featuring future pro stars like Bill Russell, Jerry West and Oscar Robertson basically just had to show up to collect the gold medal. Or as Thompson puts it: "We could close our eyes and pick a few players and beat everybody."

Even then, it was the Soviets who almost always put up the most resistance and grabbed the silver medal. And little by little they and the rest of the world have narrowed the gap — culminating in that incredible shocker at Munich.

Most American spectators of the Munich game still believe the Soviet win was gift-wrapped by the officials, who inexplicably twice turned the clock back

Michael Jordan, formerly of the University of North Carolina and now one of U.S. professional basketball's brightest stars, soars high above everyone else as the U.S. wins the gold against Spain in 1984.

Hortencia Marcari of Brazil exhibits the perfect shooting form which helps make Brazil a strong threat for a medal.

a few seconds in the closing moments, giving the Soviets a couple of extra chances. But even had the Americans won, the closeness of the score demonstrated that the days of total U.S. domination were over.

The circumstances of the loss in Munich left the United States thirsting for revenge against the Soviet team in the 1976 Olympics at Montreal. It was denied them, however, not because they failed to win the gold, but because they won it at the expense of Yugoslavia, who had upset the Soviets in the semifinals. And of course boycotts eliminated the chance for a rematch in 1980 and 1984.

But the return final now beckons, if both teams are up to the task and if nobody else spoils the party. The most likely candidate in the latter category is Yugoslavia, which, after winning the silver medal in Montreal, pulled off an even bigger shocker by knocking off the Soviets in their own backyard to win the gold in Moscow. In general, they play a physical game fairly similar to that of the Soviets, though perhaps a bit more refined. While both teams have sought far quicker players than they used to have, neither has the overall speed or mobility to stay with the Americans for a full game, so on defense they tend to fall back quickly around the basket and force the opposition to shoot from outside — a strategy that obviously can be defeated by a team with good shooters.

These three teams should divide the medals, but if there is to be an upsetter it will almost certainly come from a second trio of Brazil (which defeated the U.S. for the Pan Am Games gold medal), Spain (the silver medalist behind the Americans in 1984) and Italy. Of these, Brazil is the strongest, very close in talent to the Soviets and Yugoslavs. Another country that has been improving and could be a

Anne Donovan, one of the most dependable U.S. players, in action against the Soviets in the 1986 Goodwill Games in Moscow. Beating the experienced Soviet team provided a big boost to the confidence of the U.S. squad.

factor is China, but most observers think its team is not yet a serious contender.

Women's basketball, which only became an Olympic sport in 1976, was strictly a Soviet show the first two times, then was dominated by the United States at Los Angeles in 1984. Although the superpowers haven't had a chance to go at each other in the last two Olympics, as with the men they probably will get their chance in this year's final.

In 1976, before the women's game had really taken off in the United States, it was no contest. The U.S.S.R. just had too much size and strength, beating the Americans 122-77 and overpowering all other opposition as well.

But the Americans have made tremendous strides since Montreal, and lately their quickness and agility have prevailed more often than not—as in the Goodwill Games in Moscow two years ago where they beat the host team.

"Those victories were a big milestone for us. Playing in the Soviet Union and beating them like that gave us a tremendous lift," says this year's U.S. coach, Kay Yow.

They also led to the Soviets paying them the ultimate compliment last year of replacing their coaching staff and bringing up a number of younger, faster players to keep up with the speedy U.S. team.

"In the World Championships last year we saw a younger team," Yow says. "Obviously they had decided to get more speed and quickness."

One noticeable change is expected to be the absence of Iuliyana Semenova, the 7-foot center who dominated the women's game in the '70s and early '80s. Semenova announced her retirement last year. The Soviets have also tried to keep up with modern trends, attempting to get more movement on the court and putting more emphasis on outside shooting as opposed to their old system of just trying to get the ball in to the "tall timbers" around the basket. The result, if the teams do meet in the final, will be a game where the Americans are still somewhat faster and the Soviets somewhat bigger—but with the gaps narrowed significantly in both areas.

"I believe the 1988 Olympics will be the most competitive ever," says Yow. "The U.S. and the Soviets are always the marked teams, but China has improved tremendously."

Other teams with a shot include Bulgaria, a medalist in both 1976 and 1980; Canada, which most closely resembles the Americans in its running style of play; Brazil, whose star forward, Hortencia Marcari, may be the world's best player; Czechoslovakia, which normally can play with the best; and South Korea, which will have a huge "home court advantage" and is coming off a silver medal at Los Angeles.

The U.S. roster will include many past and present college stars, players like Anne Donovan of Old Dominion and Teresa Edwards of Georgia.

Still, the team generally winds up giving away a lot in terms of experience to its European rivals—which Yow doesn't think is necessarily all bad.

"I certainly want some experience on the team, but in other cases I want youthful enthusiasm, too," she says.

She'll certainly have that—plus plenty of speed and skill—with which to attempt to offset the perennial Soviet height advantage. It should be quite a matchup. ■

Players like 6'10" Danny Manning of Kansas, who can handle the ball with the skill of a guard, as he demonstrates in the 1987 Pan Am Games, make the U.S. heavy favorites to win the gold.

CANOE/KAYAK

by Eric Evans

For the uninitiated Olympic spectator, the sport of "canoeing" evokes images of drifting on a quiet lake in an aluminum canoe with a friend in the bow and a picnic amidships. The reality of twelve fiercely competitive Olympic canoeing and kayaking events to be contested on the man-made Han River Regatta course, 30 kilometers east of downtown Seoul, should change that. There is nothing at all peaceful about a superbly fit Olympic racer driving hard to the finish line.

....

Eric Evans placed seventh in the 1972 Olympic whitewater kayaking event and was a ten-time national kayak champion. The author of *The Kayaking Book*, he will be NBC's canoe-kayak commentator at Seoul.

Greg Barton of the U.S. is determined to show that his kayak bronze medal in the 1984 Games was no fluke. His victory in the 1000-meters at the 1987 World Championships in Germany suggests he is the man to beat at Seoul.

Olympic canoeing encompasses both canoes and kayaks. While the structural differences between the two craft are obvious — the kayak is completely closed except for a small opening called the cockpit in which the paddler sits — the technical distinction between them concerns their method of propulsion. In the canoe, the paddler kneels, propelling the laminated wood or fiberglass-composite craft with a single-bladed paddle; kayakers sit and use a double-bladed one, steering with a foot-controlled rudder.

The razor-thin kayaks are like thoroughbreds: temperamental, hard to control and happy only when pushed to top speed. The flatwater K-1, or single kayak, is approximately 17 feet long and 21 inches wide and weighs a mere 26 pounds. The two-paddler (K-2) and four-paddler (K-4) kayaks are longer, wider and heavier.

Canoe events are for men only and the craft are slightly bulkier than the kayaks. The C-1, or single canoe, is approximately 17 feet long and 30 inches wide and weighs 35 pounds, while the C-2 is slightly larger.

Nations are allowed to enter one boat per class. Similar to head-to-head rowing or swimming events, paddlers race in separate lanes on sheltered flatwater at least three meters deep. Preliminary heats cull the large fields to semifinals and then to a final limited to nine boats.

At the start of the race all boats are stationary, their bows on but not beyond the start line while their sterns are held in position. After the starting pistol has been fired, boats must stay in their lanes until the finish.

Once underway, the pace is frenetic with many kayakers stroking at well over 110 strokes per minute. The 500-meter races are less than two minutes long; the 1000-meter events take four minutes or less for both canoes and kayaks.

Winning requires a sensitive blend of strength and endurance, smooth technique and wise pacing. Paddlers train twice a day on the water for most of the

U.S. women (foreground) in the final of the K-4 in the 1984 Games, racing against Norway (middle) and Great Britain. The U.S. finished fourth.

year while off-the-water workouts include weightlifting for the crucial upper body muscles, and running, swimming or cross-country skiing for the cardiovascular system. Technique is perhaps more important than brawn and often overlooked by aspiring racers. Competitors seek to attain the utmost propulsion from each stroke while keeping the boat gliding forward as smoothly as possible; boats with more than one paddler must be particularly attuned to synchronization. Finally, there isn't a paddler in the world who can sprint all-out for 500 meters, much less 1000. Proper pacing is one of the keys to success and viewers will often see a race's early leaders over-

taken in the last 20 meters by others who expended their resources more sensibly.

Introduced as an exhibition event on the Seine River in Paris during the 1924 Olympics, flatwater canoe and kayak racing became an official event at the 1936 Berlin Olympics. Over the years Europe has been a stronghold for flatwater racing, its swiftest racers coming from the Soviet Union, East Germany, Hungary and Sweden. The best flatwater kayaker of all was Sweden's Gert Fredriksson, who garnered six gold medals over four Olympics from 1948 to 1960. Lately, paddlers from the Eastern Bloc have dominated and their success is attributed to the thousands of participating athletes who, on their way to the top, are well-funded and coached.

At the 1984 Olympics at Los Angeles, the quality of the field suffered when the Soviet Union, East Germany, Hungary and other strong canoeing nations boycotted the Games.

In their absence, traditional canoeing have-nots such as New Zealand, Australia, Canada, Spain and Denmark paddled

away with the medals. Michigan's Greg "Buck" Barton won the bronze in the K-1 1000, the first U.S. Olympic men's kayaking medal since 1936.

Barton, now 28 and living in Newport Beach, California, where he can paddle year-round, has made a clear case that his medal of '84 was legitimate. At the 1987 World Championships at Duisburg, Germany, with all the hotshot paddlers in attendance, Barton demolished the K-1 1000 field by more than three seconds in a sport where tenths of a second sometimes separate the three medal winners. Less than two months later he repeated this victory at the pre-Olympic Regatta in Seoul. His toughest competition should come from Hungary's Ferenc Csipes, Britain's Jeremy West and New Zealand's Alan Thompson.

In an unstated but palpable sense, the Seoul Games in 1988 will see the traditional canoeing powers eager to reassert their supremacy at the expense of the '84 upstarts who will be trying to prove their victories were not hollow. ∎

JUDO

by Joe Ciokin

● *Men*
60 kg. (132 lbs.)
65 kg. (143 lbs.)
71 kg. (156.5 lbs.)
78 kg. (172 lbs.)
86 kg. (189.5 lbs.)
95 kg. (209 lbs.)
95-plus kg. (over 209 lbs.)

With its violent throws and legal choke holds, no sport is more wonderfully misnamed than judo, which in Japanese means "gentle way."

There is little that is gentle about judo, which was developed in 1882 by Jigoro Kano, a Japanese teacher of physical education. Compounded of elements of jujitsu and other martial arts, judo is a demanding, occasionally brutal sport requiring both strength and agility.

When judo was first introduced into the Olympics at the Tokyo Games in 1964, it was a largely Japanese sport. With fifteen nations competing, the Japanese won three of the four events. Since then it has grown immensely in popularity; at Seoul as many as fifty nations might have athletes competing in the seven weight classes. And the Japanese, who initially dominated it, will now be hard-pressed by several countries.

Judo matches are five minutes long and take place on a 16 x 16-meter mat surrounded by a red border, indicating a danger area about one meter in width. A penalty is assessed if a contestant intentionally steps outside—or pushes his opponent outside—the danger area.

Judokas, as the competitors are called, wear heavy cotton uniforms tied at the waist by a cloth belt indicating rank and by either a red or white sash to help scorekeepers and officials distinguish between them.

Joe Ciokon, freelance writer and retired U.S. Navy broadcast journalist, has been a national and international competitor and coach for national judo teams.

Following the referee's shout of "Hajime" (begin), the Judokas try to throw each other to the mat, grappling in the process to get effective holds on their opponents. Tripping and employing the opponent's own momentum to get him off-balance and vulnerable to a throw are part of the forty techniques basic to the sport.

A match can be won in a variety of ways, but the primary objective for all players is to score an ippon, which, like a knockout in boxing or a pin in wrestling, ends the match immediately. An ippon is scored when the opponent is hurled onto his back with considerable force, execution and control; when the opponent is held on his back for thirty seconds; or when a choke or armbar forces the opponent to surrender.

The second-best award is the waza ari which carries half-point credit. The waza ari is earned for a throw that is not quite perfect or for a hold of more than twenty-five but less than thirty seconds. Scoring two waza aris equals an ippon, and thus ends the match.

A yuko is awarded for a throw to the mat that is judged not quite as complete as a waza ari or for a pin that is held for twenty to twenty-five seconds. A koka is awarded for a throw that lacks force and speed or for a pin of between ten and twenty seconds. One waza ari will beat any number of yukos, and one yuko will beat any number of kokas.

Penalties in judo parallel scoring. Thus hansoku-make, which is called for dangerous throws or poor sportsmanship, is like an ippon in that it results in the end of the match. Two calls of keikoku, which is a warning of serious possible offense or stepping out of bounds on purpose, also produce an instant loss, just as two waza aris deliver a victory. A waza ari can also be combined with a keikoku to total an ippon and end the match.

If a match goes the full five minutes, the referee declares the winner based on accumulated scores. If there has been no score or if the match is tied, the referee requests the two judges' decisions, which they declare by holding up either a red or white flag, corresponding to the sash color of the contestant they prefer. In the case of a split decision, the referee has the deciding vote.

Several changes have occurred in the world judo scene since the Los Angeles Games of 1984, most notably in the decision to introduce women's competition into the current Olympics as a demonstration sport. To accommodate the women's event, the men's "open" weight division has been dropped.

The challenge to traditional Japanese judo strength should come primarily from the U.S.S.R., France and the U.S. While the Soviets have for a number of years been solidly entrenched as the world's runner-up, they may well be displaced by the French, whose program has been steadily improving.

Most startling of all has been the development of the U.S. team. At the 1987 World Championships in West Germany, the U.S. stunned the judo community by winning its first men's World Championship gold medal. Mike Swain, 27, handled the toughest competition in the 71 kg. division, including Toshihiko Koga of Japan. In the final he defeated the favored Marc Alexandre of France.

Hawaiian-born Kevin Asano, 24, was the surprise bronze medalist in the 60 kg. class in Germany. He lost in the semifinals to eventual gold medalist Shinji Hosokawa of Japan in a match many people thought he deserved to win. Asano has been gaining important international experience the last two years and will be a serious contender at Seoul.

Others with a chance to medal for the rapidly improving U.S. squad include Jason Morris at 78 kg. and Steve Cohen in the 95 kg. division. ■

Mike Swain, the best U.S. hope for a gold medal in Seoul, on his way to winning the 1987 World Championships in the 71-kilogram division.

VOLLEYBALL

by Jonathan Lee

● *Men's event*

● *Women's event*

There was a time when American volleyball players cringed at the thought of a match with Japan, shuddered when the Cubans were mentioned and winced at the prospect of battle with the Soviets. Lowly U.S. teams were powerless against alien volleyball aggression.

It was tough to swallow. After all, volleyball had been invented in Massachusetts in 1895 and exported by American GIs as a post-war goodwill offering to war-ravaged Europe and Asia. But throughout the 60s and 70s, American players found themselves sitting in the grandstands watching other world powers sort out Olympic medals.

But no more. Today the U.S. men are not only the defenders of the Olympic gold, they're odds-on favorites to repeat in '88. And the American women, despite a complete turnover of personnel since their '84 silver medal, are still in the thick of the medal quest in Seoul.

The turnabout of American fortunes has been as dramatic as the transformation of the game itself.

Volleyball started out a simple game, casual recreation, a perfect activity for picnics and beach parties. Net heights, team size and court dimensions were determined by those eager to play. Games usually ended when the hot dogs were done.

Organized volleyball has some basic rules that have remained intact through the years. There are still two hits permitted by the six-person team before it must hit the ball over the net (7'11⅝" for men, 7'4½" for women) and into the opponent's court. The same player cannot hit the ball twice in succession. Only the serving

Jonathan Lee, former editor of *Volleyball* magazine, is a staff writer for *Volleyball Monthly*. He has traveled around the world to cover Olympic, World Cup and Pan American Games volleyball competition.

team can score. If the receiving team wins a rally, it gets the serve and the opportunity to score. Fifteen points wins the game, provided it is by a two-point margin. The first team to win three games wins the match.

What started out simple did not remain so. As various countries adapted the game to their native skills and national characteristics, volleyball underwent many major facelifts. Players got bigger and quicker, techniques and tactics more refined. Instead of being merely a means of getting the ball into play, the serve became a weapon. Today the jump serves of most top teams clear the net by inches and travel at nearly 80 mph.

The reception of serves has become such a critical part of play that most teams rely on two or three specialists who swear off all worldly vices and dedicate themselves, body and soul, to serve reception. They cover the entire court while the other players stand in corners waiting to break from their starting positions into an attack mode. Passers must handle the ball on their extended forearms and send it to the front of the court. The second team contact, called "the set," has become a test of quickness and deception as the setter attempts to outmaneuver the big blockers stationed across the net. The setter contacts the ball with his fingertips, feeding pre-planned sets to big bombers who attack the ball from front row positions, or to back row spikers who must take off from behind the three-meter line. When these attackers lower the boom, the ball can travel at speeds up to 100 mph.

While the Soviets developed an impervious blocking strategy at net that kept most teams cowering in submission, defensive techniques were also perfected by the Japanese men and women who practiced diving full-length on the hardwood floor to return the ball. A quick attack, designed by Japanese innovators, saw airborne spikers get sets before blockers could react.

The Polish refined the Asian quick attack by adding screens and fakes. They confounded even the huge Russians for a

Steve Timmons, one of the reasons the U.S. is favored in the Olympics, tries to power the ball past the formidable Soviet blocking duo of Aleksander Savin and Jaroslav Antonov at the 1986 Goodwill Games in Moscow.

World Championship in '74 and an Olympic gold in '76.

And through all the evolution, the American inventors of the sport stood back and watched in obscurity. The U.S. had the athletes but not the organization, financial backing or training programs to make them competitive. The men didn't qualify for the Olympics from 1972 to 1980.

When the men finished 19th in the '78 World Championships and lost to the Dominican Republic in the '79 Olympic

qualifying tournament, the U.S. decided something had to be done.

In 1981 a full-time national training center was established in California, where most of the best players lived. Within three years, the recruitment, training and competitive schedule had turned everybody's patsy into the elite squad on earth.

After winning the 1984 Olympics (without, of course, the Soviet presence), the U.S. men completed the sweep of the triple crown with victories in the 1985 World Cup and the 1986 World Championships. The U.S. not only made it to the top, it has stayed there, winning every major international event it has entered. In 1987 the Americans defeated the Soviets in the finals of both the Savvine Cup in Moscow and the USA Cup in Los Angeles.

Head coach Marv Dunphy explains what has kept the Americans number one. "We started the National Training Center with some unique competitive athletes. Doug (Beal) developed and prepared them for that win in L.A. And even though we've lost Doug and some of those early key players, people like Karch Kiraly, Craig Buck and Steve Timmons have enabled us to stay on top. We are still the most experienced team in the world."

"Our continued success is a tribute to the program," observes Kiraly, generally considered the best all-around player in the game. "Despite the retirement of two of the world's best, Dusty Dvorak (at setter) and Pat Powers (at outside hitter), we've been able to develop replacements who are now experienced enough to blend in with the veterans and keep us where we are."

The Americans will be tested by the flamboyant French in their competitive Olympic pool. France is currently rated number four worldwide and features a diversified attack. Each spiker is capable of hitting many types of sets to catch blockers off balance. "This is a more complicated style than ours, and a little riskier," says Kiraly, "but it's fun to watch when it's working."

Although they are much weaker than they have been, the Soviets have a distinguished volleyball tradition which must always be respected. They have been to international volleyball what the New York Yankees once were to baseball, the Celtics to basketball—the dominant force. The current Soviet squad has suffered from numerous retirements, but it is still a powerful threat to the U.S. and better than the rest.

Testing the Soviets will be Bulgaria and Brazil, Olympic silver medalists in '80 and '84 respectively and third and fourth in the '86 World Championships. Both teams have world-class strength and legitimate shots at Olympic medals at Seoul.

The announced boycott by Cuba will diminish the meaning of the medals in the men's competition, for Cuba was considered only a thin slice below the Soviets and a certain medalist. Without the Cubans, others may have an easier time, but all the spectators will suffer. Cuba features high-flying NBA style

The absence of the Cuban women, "perhaps the best women's volleyball team ever," according to U.S. coach Terry Liskevych, will give the U.S. a good shot at the gold.

athletes that are as close as Cuba comes to having a space program. They show up regularly on U.S. radar screens trained on Cuba, but will not show up at Seoul.

An even bigger loss is the Cuban women, who finished second to China in the 1986 World Championships but have since avenged that loss several times. "They are," says U.S. head coach Terry Liskevych, "the best team in the world, by far, not even close. They may be the best women's volleyball team ever."

So the Olympics could well be a test to see who's second best. Without Cuban dominance, the Chinese, Peruvian, East German, Japanese, Soviet and American women step right into Olympic gold contention.

The American women rose to respectability before the men. In 1980 they not only won Olympic qualification but were expected to win a medal in the Moscow Games. The U.S. boycott dashed that ambition and the powerful but aging Americans settled for a silver in 1984 behind China's gold.

Since then the U.S. team, with a few exceptions, has experienced a complete personnel turnover in a game where experience is vital. "We had two goals for 1987," says Liskevych, "to beat one of the world's top three and to qualify for the Olympics. Beating China (ranked No. 2 behind Cuba) in the Japan Cup was a huge win for us and a silver medal in the Olympic qualifier in Havana gave us an Olympic berth. We're on target despite our youth and have a good shot at a medal in Seoul."

Without the Cubans, the Chinese appear the strongest team. They have seven of their top nine players back from their 1984 Olympic triumph and have added World Cup ('85) and World Championship ('86) gold medals to their treasure trove. Not bad for a team whose first taste of Olympic competition was at Los Angeles. They are quick, superbly trained and well-accustomed to the pressures of international play.

The East Germans still present a slow but powerful brand of volleyball that carried them to a victory over the Soviet Union in the European Championships.

That upset left the Soviets to claw for Olympic qualification at a May tournament in Forli, Italy.

The Peruvian women have the ability to beat every team in the field. At the last big pre-Olympic showdown, the '87 Japan Cup, they took first place. Cuba was not competing, but China, the U.S. and the rest of the world's elite were. Seoul will feature the same menu, and the small but exceedingly tough Peruvians may just eat it up.

Whoever wins, every match will reveal the power, quickness and spectacle that is modern volleyball. It will be clear why volleyball has grown to be one of the world's most popular sports. And Americans will be able to hold their heads up proudly when people mention the game invented in their own backyard. ∎

Karch Kiraly, who was honored in 1986 by the International Volleyball Federation as the World's Best Volleyball Player, gets set to serve against Canada in the USA Cup. A pre-med major in college, Kiraly keeps putting off medical school to continue playing volleyball.

ARCHERY

by Mike James

●**Men**
Individual
Team
●**Women**
Individual
Team

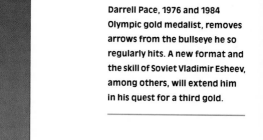

Darrell Pace, 1976 and 1984 Olympic gold medalist, removes arrows from the bullseye he so regularly hits. A new format and the skill of Soviet Vladimir Esheev, among others, will extend him in his quest for a third gold.

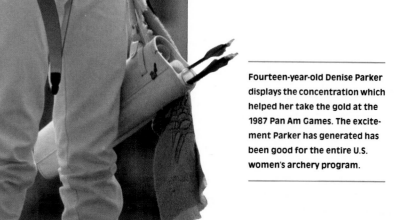

D arrell Pace stepped to the line on the final day of archery competition in the 1984 Olympics at Los Angeles with a lead so massive he almost could have wrapped up the gold medal blindfolded.

Pace, a runaway gold medalist in '76, was so relaxed, so far ahead of the next archer after the first three days of the meet that he even took a break to chat with reporters midway through the final round. Tension is inherent in this quiet sport, but this climax was hardly high drama. Pace won the gold by a huge margin, the outcome essentially determined before the final day, the score the only question.

That won't happen this year.

In the Seoul Olympics, archers will compete under a new format designed to increase suspense as the competition progresses.

In the past, medals were determined by the best score over a four-day period. Competitors shot 288 arrows at four distances — 90, 70, 50 and 30 meters for men; 70, 60, 50 and 30 for women.

The target, about 31 inches in diameter for the 50- and 30-meter events and 48 inches for the others, has ten rings. The outside ring is worth one point, the center ring bullseye (which is only about five inches in diameter on the large target and three inches on the small) worth ten. So a perfect score for 288 arrows would be 2,880 points.

Pace won in '84 by 52 points over U.S. silver medalist Rick McKinney. These two

Mike James, assistant sports editor of *The Los Angeles Times* Orange County bureau, has been a sportswriter and editor since 1978, and has contributed numerous sports articles to national publications.

archers have dominated since the mid-1970s, capturing five world target championships between them. Pace's 2,616 total points broke the Olympic record he had set in '76.

This year, under the Grand FITA (Federation Internationale de Tir a l'Arc) format, archers will compete in elimination rounds. After 144 arrows, the field will be cut to twenty-four. That group starts from scratch with thirty-six arrows and archers with the top eighteen scores advance. In subsequent rounds of thirty-six arrows, the field will be cut to twelve and then to the final eight.

In the final round, the archers shoot another thirty-six arrows, nine each beginning at 30 meters and working their way up. A runaway victory will be almost impossible, particularly because the final nine arrows will be shot at the greatest distance, which, of course, has the greatest margin of error.

Pace, 31, from Ohio, is the only archer to have won two Olympic gold medals. He isn't wild about the new format.

Fourteen-year-old Denise Parker displays the concentration which helped her take the gold at the 1987 Pan Am Games. The excitement Parker has generated has been good for the entire U.S. women's archery program.

"Before, you had to be great for four consecutive days; now you're just making the cut," he says. "If a man shoots 250 arrows in the middle better than I do, by God, he deserves to win."

The new format was in use at the 1987 World Championships. The Soviet Union's Vladimir Esheev, who won that event, is an extremely strong competitor in the Grand FITA format, as is Jay Barrs of the U.S., who finished third in the 1987 World Championships. West Germany's Andreas Lippoldt, who finished second in the World Championships, is also a solid Grand FITA shooter.

Japan's Takayoshi Matsushita, who finished fourth in the '84 Games, Finland's Tomi Poikolainen, who was fifth, Sweden's Göran Bjerendal (sixth) and South Korea's Koo Ja-Chung (eighth) are others who have experienced substantial international success.

The strength of the women's field lies primarily in South Korea, the Soviet Union and China. China's Xiangjun Ma is the '87 World Champion. Hee-Kyung Wang is one of several Koreans shooting well enough to win. Ludmila Arzhannikova and Elena Marfel are two top Soviets.

The United States' hopes, particularly for the future, may rest with Denise Parker, a 14-year-old wunderkind from Utah. Parker was the gold medalist in the '87 Pan Am Games and is providing women's archery in the United States with a shot of adrenaline.

"Denise has a regular weight-training program and a real training regimen," said Sheri Rhodes, coach of the U.S. men's and women's teams. "Our status in the world has dropped a bit, but she's one reason there is more dedication on the part of other [women] archers these days. Face it, when you've been shooting competitively for fifteen years and you get beat by a kid who has been shooting for three and a half, it's not the kind of thing you had planned on."

Archery has often been called the quiet sport. Meets don't usually attract crowds. The subtle sounds on the greensward almost define the sport: the whistle signaling the moment the archers may fire, the release of the bowstrings and the thumps of the arrows, traveling up to 230 feet per second, finding their targets. The cheerleading comes pretty much from within. But another change in Seoul may alter that, too.

For the first time, there will be a separate team competition, in which each of three team members shoots 144 arrows, the total of their three scores determining the medals. This is a popular change with the archers, who say they look forward to rooting for their teammates once the silent tension of individual shooting has ended.

Of course, it's little wonder that U.S. men like the idea as much as anyone. Pace, McKinney and Barrs shattered the world team record in the '87 Pan Am Games. ■

TEAM HANDBALL

by Mark Wright

● *Men's event*

● *Women's event*

For the average American sports fan lacking experience with the game, team handball is a little like watching a popular American movie dubbed into a foreign language. Much of it will seem quite familiar and at times the viewer will, almost by instinct, surmise all of what's going on. At other times, though,

....

Mark Wright, former captain of the U.S. men's national team handball team, has produced videos and written extensively on the sport.

things will be hopelessly confused, the viewer befuddled by the sport's strategy, overwhelmed by its speed and contact. The good news is that familiarity usually wins out rather quickly and even novice spectators can learn to enjoy the sport by the end of their first game.

A little background can help. Team handball, developed simultaneously in Denmark and Germany around the turn of the century, made a one-time Olympic appearance in 1936 and returned for good in 1972 for men and in 1976 for women. Though still virtually unknown in the U.S., the sport is played around the world by millions of participants of all ages. In fact, the case could be made that team

handball is the second most popular team sport in the world, behind only soccer.

Although most Americans don't know the sport, those who do have described it in interesting ways: "Basketball with goals instead of hoops," "ice hockey with tennis shoes and no ice," "water polo on land," and "soccer with hands." It speaks to the special quality of team handball that they all suggest some part of its feeling and action.

Basically, it is a game of putting a ball into a net. This is done by two teams of seven players (six court players and a goalie), who play thirty-minute halves on a 20 x 40-meter court (about 15 feet longer than a basketball court). The

Cindy Stinger of the U.S., one of the most accomplished players in the world, tries to break free from the grasp of a Brazilian player in the 1987 Pan Am Games.

The last line of defense is, of course, the goalie who, like a quarterback or pitcher, can make a mediocre team good, a good team great.

The qualities required to excel as a team handball player are precisely those which American athletes tend to possess in abundance: strong throwing arm, speed, jumping ability, substantial size and mental quickness. Experts in the game shudder to consider American team handball potential. Picture Tom Seaver in his prime, with a head of steam, leaping up and launching a high fastball. Now put a team handball in his hand instead of a baseball and you have the image that the best European coaches have been conjuring up — and dreading — for years.

That day has not arrived yet, but American chances in Seoul are the best they've ever been. The U.S. men qualified by beating Cuba in last summer's Pan Am Games. The return of several veterans from the 1984 Games, including 36-year-old team-captain Joe Story, along with the coaching mastery of Branislav Pokrajac, coach of the 1984 Olympic champion Yugoslavian team, gives the U.S. unprecedented hopes for 1988.

Coached by Mihaly (Misha) Faludi, who previously coached the Hungarian men's Olympic team, the U.S. women's team qualified for Seoul by beating Canada soundly in the qualifying Pan Am Games. It is led by veteran Cindy Stinger, who celebrated 1987 by being named Most Valuable Player at the U.S. Nationals, the U.S.A. Cup and the Pan American Games. She is truly a player who ranks among the world's best. The women will find their toughest competition coming from the Soviet Union, Yugoslavia and Norway.

Whatever the outcome of the contests in Seoul, the sport can only prosper from the media and television coverage that will undoubtedly be generated during the Olympics. Having labored in virtual seclusion for the past thirty years in this country, team handball players await an American public at long last knowledgeable and appreciative. When that day arrives, Americans will be ready to compete at the highest international level. ∎

Ringed by the defensive players who cannot step inside the six-meter line in front of their goal, Sergei Karsakijevic of the U.S.S.R. launches a shot in the 1986 Goodwill Games in Moscow.

leather-paneled ball, about the size of a junior soccer ball, is moved by dribbling and passing, just as in basketball. Two basic rules govern the movement and tempo of the game: A player standing still can hold the ball for no longer than three seconds, while a player on the move can take up to three steps before he must dribble, pass or shoot the ball. Set plays are designed to create opportunities for offensive players to shoot either over or between the defensive players, who must stay at least six meters away from the goal.

The defense, meanwhile, attempts to control the offense and prevent it from scoring. In that effort, defensive players are allowed to use a certain amount of contact, roughly that found in hockey.

RHYTHMIC GYMNASTICS

by Dwight Normile

●*Women*
All-around

Rhythmic gymnastics is a sport whose time has come. While this elegant sport made its Olympic debut at the 1984 Games, the Eastern Bloc boycott reduced its impact on the viewing public. The Seoul Olympics should change all that.

Originated by the ancient Greeks, rhythmic gymnastic competitions were held in East European countries for thirty years before the sport was officially recognized in 1962 by the Federation of International Gymnastics.

The goal of the rhythmic gymnast is to create pure, harmonious movement exclusive of acrobatics, performing with four types of equipment: rope, hoop, clubs and ribbon. (The fifth apparatus, ball, is used in the group event, which has not yet been accepted for the Olympic agenda. Every other year a different apparatus is rotated out of the individual competition to the group event.)

Each apparatus is of a standardized size, weight and material, and may be any color except gold, silver or bronze. Movements to look for, in addition to throwing and catching, include the following:

Rope: jumps with rope open or folded, swinging and circling.

Clubs: large and small circles, rhythmical tapping, swings.

Hoop: turns, spins, rotations on floor and around hand or body parts.

Ribbon: snakes, spirals, large and small circles.

The apparatus should never stop moving, except for accents, and the gymnast must include movements at three levels: in the air (leaping), standing upright (dance) and on the floor (rolling).

....

Dwight Normile, editor since 1982 of *International Gymnast*, is a former national gymnastics competitor and judge.

The maximum score is 10, and each routine must contain at least four elements of superior difficulty and four of medium difficulty (upgraded from L.A. '84 where two superiors and six mediums were required). An example of a superior element in a clubs exercise, for instance, would be two consecutive leaps by the gymnast while the clubs are in the air.

All routines are 60 to 90 seconds in length and performed on a 40 x 40-foot carpeted floor to the musical accompaniment of one instrument. The combined score of all four exercises determines the all-around champion.

Six judges plus a head judge evaluate the two contestants from each country on technical excellence, difficulty of routine, choreography, harmony with the music and use of the floor space. Loss of points for dropping the apparatus varies with the number of musical beats used to recover it. Further deductions occur if a gymnast has to leave the floor boundary to retrieve her apparatus. Acrobatic feats such as flips, cartwheels and handsprings are prohibited.

Today's rhythmic gymnasts are extraordinary athletes. To begin with, the sport requires a mastery of ballet, a demanding discipline itself. The gymnast must be both strong and flexible in order to display effectively the various body positions required by the sport.

Second, the intricate handling of the different apparatuses demands fine eye-hand coordination, not to mention intense concentration. These gymnasts develop an ambidexterity common to jugglers, only they are leaping and pirouetting during their spectacular feats.

The third quality a successful rhythmic gymnast must possess is the capacity to project feeling. Each routine tends to have an emotional coherence, and whether she is expressing a dramatic or romantic mood, the gymnast should be able to convey it through her movements.

Together, then, the successful rhythmic gymnast must be a dancer, gymnast, juggler, magician and actor rolled into one.

Marina Lobach of the Soviet Union seems effortlessly connected to her ribbon as she leaps through the air. She will in fact exert enormous effort at Seoul as she strives to upset World Champion Bianca Panova of Bulgaria.

The great rhythmic masters tend to be Bulgarians and Soviets, and the overall excellence of today's competitors makes it increasingly difficult for judges to find distinctions between them. At the 1987 World Championships, for example, while gold-medalist Bianca Panova of Bulgaria scored a 10 each time she performed, each of her two teammates who were tied for second earned two perfect scores. Although Panova will be favored to win at Seoul, one small slip could leave her out of the medals altogether.

If she does earn the gold, it will be another demonstration of the skill of Bulgarian national coach Neschka Robeva, whose gymnasts have dominated the sport for the last ten years. Any non-Bulgarian winner would mark a great upset, though Soviet Marina Lobach and newcomer Anna Kotchneva have the talent and drive to challenge Panova.

Regardless of who wins, nothing can obscure the sheer beauty of rhythmic gymnastics. The Seoul Olympics will provide the first real opportunity for people around the world to witness this marvelous sport at its best, and its popularity could very well explode across the Western world. ■

SYNCHRONIZED SWIMMING

by Karen Crouse

● **Women's Events**
Solo
Duet

Almost from the moment Tracie Ruiz-Conforto learned her first figure in a pool in Bothell, Washington, she aspired to be just like Esther Williams, the legendary water ballet queen of the silver screen.

In that respect, Ruiz-Conforto was like any other pint-sized synchronized swimmer in the early 1970s. With no Olympic heroines to fuel their competitive dreams, youngsters like the then-nine-year-old Ruiz had little choice but to make the glitter and glamour of Hollywood the stuff of their fantasies.

The 1984 Olympics, though, spawned a new generation of synchronized swimmers, for whom Ruiz-Conforto is now the star. At Los Angeles, the 21-year-old University of Arizona student with cover girl looks became a role model for youngsters from Auckland to Zurich by winning the first two Olympic gold medals ever awarded in the sport. First she teamed with longtime partner Candy Costie to win the duet crown. Then, displaying moves that were as athletic as they were dazzling, she captured first in the solo, an event added to the Olympic program at the last minute in the wake of the Soviet-led boycott.

In 1988 Ruiz-Conforto will try to win the gold again after a two-year retirement following her 1984 victory.

The sport in which she will compete at Seoul has little to do with the languorous moves of water ballet, with which it is sometimes mistakenly compared. Synchronized swimming is a rigorous and exacting sport, demanding genuine athletic skills and years of dedicated training.

Both solo and duet events consist of two parts: compulsory figures and a routine (four minutes for duet, three and one-half for solo).

··

Karen Crouse is a freelance writer who previously covered sports for the *Peninsula Times Tribune* in Palo Alto, California.

While hardly exciting to watch, the six designated figures the swimmers must perform before the judges are critical. As the world's best synchronized swimmers tend to be equally talented in the routines, success in the figures is often the difference between the gold and silver.

The figures, drawn at random from a possible thirty-six, are evaluated on a scale of 0-10 by the judges. Every part of each figure is carefully observed: technical perfection of every movement is the goal for which all strive.

The judges look for much more in the solo and duet routines than simple technical excellence. For example:

● *Time spent underwater:* The longer a swimmer spends under water, the harder her routine is deemed and the more points she is likely to garner. It is not uncommon for a swimmer to spend the first minute with her smile buried beneath the surface.

● *Vertical extension:* The best swimmers can propel themselves upward until the water line is below their navels.

● *General style:* This includes the swimmer's ability to synchronize moves with the music; the variety of moves she performs and their difficulty; her success in utilizing the whole pool; her presentation, and her rapport with the audience and judges.

In the duet, synchronization between partners is also a major consideration as the two swimmers strive to perform as mirror images.

If Ruiz-Conforto is to repeat as Olympic solo winner, she will have to beat Canadian Carolyn Waldo, the 1984 silver medalist who has become the world's best synchronized swimmer. Winner of

Tracie Ruiz-Conforto and her partner, Candy Costie, display the harmony and grace underwater which earned them the gold medal for the duet in the 1984 Games. Ruiz-Conforto will compete this year only in the solo event, in which she will try to capture her second consecutive gold.

the solo competition at the 1987 FINA World Cup in Cairo, Waldo, along with teammate Michelle Cameron, will also be strong in duet.

The United States will be represented in the duet by the four-time national champion pair of Karen and Sarah Josephson.

The Josephsons, 24-year-old identical twins from Connecticut, finished second to Waldo and Cameron at the FINA Cup, but by a much closer score than their second-place finish a year earlier in the World Championships at Madrid. Their showing at the FINA Cup gave U.S. national coach Charlotte Davis cause for optimism.

"If you believe in Sarah's and Karen's progress, then you'd have to put your money on them," Davis said. "But really, I just think it's going to be an exciting competition. I think it's going to come

The U.S. national champions, identical twins Karen and Sarah Josephson, will challenge Canadian World Champions Carolyn Waldo and Michelle Cameron in the duet event.

down to whoever's the best on that particular day."

Besides Waldo, Cameron and the Americans, other strong swimmers in the solo event are Muriel Hermine, a part-time model from France, Mikako Kotani of Japan and Karin Singer of Switzerland. In

the duet, the French team of Hermine and Karine Schuler, the Swiss pair of Edith Boss and Singer, and the Soviet entry of Tatiana Titova and Irina Zhukova are ones to watch. ■

TENNIS and TABLE TENNIS

by Larry Eldridge

Tennis and Table tennis

●*Men*
Singles
Doubles

●*Women*
Singles
Doubles

Tennis and table tennis are the new kids on the block at these Olympics—the former returning to the Games after an absence of more than sixty years, the latter making its debut as an Olympic sport. And many of the world's top players will be vying for the twelve medals up for grabs in each sport in the twelve-day competition.

In tennis, the major restriction on eligibility is that players must have competed in their countries' Davis Cup or Federation Cup matches in 1987 or 1988. Although this eliminates some top players, it still permits others such as recent Wimbledon champions Pat Cash of Australia and West Germany's Boris Becker as well as Steffi Graf, who has emerged as the world's top female player, to compete.

The playing surface in Seoul is extremely fast—"like linoleum," according to some of those who have tested it—and will thus favor hard-serving grass court-type players rather than those whose game is better suited to slower clay surfaces.

Cash and Becker both fit into the former category, as do Tim Mayotte of the United States and Stefan Edberg of Sweden, who won the 1984 competition at Los Angeles where tennis was a demonstration sport. Edberg's countryman Mats Wilander, though he originally gained fame as a clay court player, has shown in the last couple of years that he can handle fast surfaces, too, and is expected to be a contender.

Without the challenge of Navratilova and Evert, Graf is expected to add the 1988 Olympic championship to the demonstration gold she won at L.A. Pam Shriver of the United States, an excellent grass court player, may be her top foe,

while Argentina's Gabriela Sabatini also appears capable of handling the fast surface.

In all, there will be four Olympic tennis events—men's singles (64 players), women's singles (48), men's doubles (32 pairs) and women's doubles (a minimum of eight pairs). Each country is permitted to enter three players in each singles

event and one pair in each doubles event.

Americans Ken Flach and Robert Seguso are the probable men's doubles favorites, with Australia (Cash and John Fitzgerald) and France (Guy Forget and Yannick Noah) the apparent top challengers.

Graf and Claudia Kohde-Kilsh should battle it out with Shriver and Elise Burgin for the women's doubles gold.

Table tennis offers the same four events and also features most of the world's top players, headed by the Chinese, who have dominated the sport in recent years. Foremost among the men is Jiang Jialiang, the first player since the mid-'60s to win two men's World Championship singles titles in a row. On the women's side, young superstar Dai Lili and her teammate, He Zhili, may well finish 1-2 and are heavy favorites to take the doubles gold.

While the Chinese are certainly the strongest team—in the last two World Championships the Chinese have won six of the seven gold medals each time—there are athletes from other countries capable of beating the Chinese in individual matches, and South Korea defeated China in the Asian Games.

The top challenger among the men is expected to be Jan-Ove Waldner of Sweden, who lost to Jiang in the World Championship final last year. Yugoslavia, Poland and Japan also have strong men's teams. The North American entrants include Gideon Joe Ng, a Canadian of Chinese extraction, and U.S. representative Sean O'Neill.

Traditional women's powers in addition to China include South Korea, Hungary, Holland, the Soviet Union and Japan. The American representative, ironically, is In Sook Bhushan, who will be returning to the country from which she emigrated in 1975.

Table tennis can be played in a variety of styles, though lately most top players tend to favor attack over defense. The Chinese are the quintessential fast-attack practitioners, staying close to the table (two to five feet away), relying on short, sharp, counter-drive type strokes, and try-ing to perform either a three-ball (serve, return and putaway) or at most a five-ball kill. Another major style, emphasizing slicing the ball to generate tremendous topspin, is best done by the Swedes. A traditional defensive style, involving chopping strokes with underspin, has become rare in men's competition and is even beginning to disappear from top-flight women's play.

This is easy enough to understand when one realizes that the ball in flight has been clocked as fast at 104 mph. To get an idea how quickly a defensive player must react to this speed, think about facing Nolan Ryan or Dwight Gooden—then remember that a baseball pitcher is standing 60 feet away from the batter, while the table is only nine feet long. ■

Former Wimbledon champion Boris Becker of West Germany will use his acrobatic return skills effectively on the fast surface at Seoul as tennis returns to the Olympics.

The 1987 singles World Champion, He Zhili, is part of a powerful women's team from the People's Republic of China.

OLYMPIC GOLD CHAMPIONS*

FOUR OR MORE GOLD MEDALS • 1896-1984

SPORT/Athlete	Nation	#	Games
ARCHERY			
Hubert Van Innis	BEL	6	'00, '20
ATHLETICS/TRACK			
Paavo Nurmi	FIN	9	'20–'28
Alvin Kraenzlein	USA	4	'00
Melvin Sheppard	USA	4	'08, '12
Johannes Kolehmainen	FIN	4	'12, '20
Jesse Owens (1 in field)	USA	3/1	'36
Fannie Blankers-Koen	HOL	4	'48
Harrison Dillard	USA	4	'48, '52
Emil Zatopek	TCH	4	'48, '52
Betty Cuthbert	AUS	4	'56, '64
Lasse Viren	FIN	4	'72, '76
Barbel Wockel	GDR	4	'76, '80
Carl Lewis (1 in field)	USA	3/1	'84
ATHLETICS/FIELD			
Ray Ewry	USA	8	'00–'08
Al Oerter	USA	4	'56–'68
CANOE/KAYAK			
Gert Fredriksson	SWE	6	'48–'60
Vladimir Morozov	URS	4	'64–'76
DIVING			
Patricia McCormick	USA	4	'52, '56
EQUESTRIAN			
Hans Winkler	FRG	5	'56–'72
Reiner Klimke	FRG	5	'64–'84
C. F. Pahud deMortanges	HOL	4	'24–'32
Henri St. Cyr	SWE	4	'52, '56
FENCING			
Aladar Gerevich	HUN	7	'32–'60
Nedo Nadi	ITA	6	'12, '20
Pál Kovács	HUN	6	'36–'60
Edoardo Mangiarotti	ITA	6	'36–'60
Rudolf Karpati	HUN	6	'48–'60
Ramón Fonst	CUB	4	'00, '04
Jeno Fuchs	HUN	4	'08, '12
Lucien Gaudin	FRA	4	'24, '28
Christian d'Oriola	FRA	4	'48–'56
Giuseppe Delfino	ITA	4	'52–'60
Carlo Pavesi	ITA	4	'52–'60
Gyozo Kulcsar	HUN	4	'64–'72

FENCING (cont'd)	Nation	#	Games
Yelena Novikova-Belova	URS	4	'68–'76
Viktor Sidiak	URS	4	'68–'80
Viktor Krovopuskov	URS	4	'76, '80
GYMNASTICS			
Larissa Latynina	URS	9	'56–'64
Sawao Kato	JPN	8	'68–'76
Viktor Chukarin	URS	7	'52, '56
Boris Shakhlin	URS	7	'56–'64
Vera Caslavska	TCH	7	'64, '68
Nikolai Andrianov	URS	7	'72–'80
Akinori Nakayama	JPN	6	'68, '72
Agnes Keleti	HUN	5	'52, '56
Polina Astakhova	URS	5	'56–'64
Takashi Ono	JPN	5	'56–'64
Yukio Endo	JPN	5	'60–'68
Mitsuo Tsukahara	JPN	5	'68–'76
Nadia Comaneci	ROM	5	'76, '80
Nelli Kim	URS	5	'76, '80
Anton Heida	USA	4	'04
George Miez	SUI	4	'28, 36
Valentin Muratov	URS	4	'52, '56
Lyudmila Tourischeva	URS	4	'68–'76
Olga Korbut	URS	4	'72, '76
Ecaterina Szabo	ROM	4	'84
SHOOTING			
Morris Fisher	USA	5	'20, '24
Ole A. Lilloe-Olsen	NOR	5	'20, '24
SWIMMING			
Mark Spitz	USA	9	'68, '72
Johnny Weissmuller	USA	5	'24, '28
Don Schollander	USA	5	'64, '68
Charles Daniels	USA	4	'04, '08
Dawn Fraser	AUS	4	'56–'64
Murray Rose	AUS	4	'56, '60
Roland Matthes	GDR	4	'68, '72
Kornelia Ender	GDR	4	'76
John Naber	USA	4	'76
WATER POLO			
Paul Radmilovic (1 in swim.)	GBR	3/1	'08–'20
YACHTING			
Paul Elvstrom	DEN	4	'48–'60

*Includes discontinued events; excludes 1906.

▨ Men   ▨ Women

OLYMPIC COUNTRY CODES

Code	Country	Code	Country
AFG	Afghanistan	KEN	Kenya
AHO	Neth. Antilles	KOR	South Korea
ALG	Algeria	KSA	Saudi Arabia
AND	Andorra	KUW	Kuwait
ANG	Angola	LAO	Laos
ANT	Antigua	LBA	Libya
ARG	Argentina	LBR	Liberia
ARU	Aruba	LES	Lesotho
AUS	Australia	LIB	Lebanon
AUT	Austria	LIE	Liechtenstein
BAH	Bahamas	LUX	Luxembourg
BAN	Bangladesh	MAD	Madagascar
BAR	Barbados	MAL	Malaysia
BEL	Belgium	MAR	Morocco
BEN	Benin	MAW	Malawi
BER	Bermuda	MDV	Maldives
BHU	Bhutan	MEX	Mexico
BIR	Burma	MGL	Mongolia
BIZ	Belize	MLI	Mali
BOL	Bolivia	MLT	Malta
BOT	Botswana	MON	Monaco
BRA	Brazil	MOZ	Mozambique
BRN	Bahrain	MRI	Mauritius
BRU	Brunei	MTN	Mauritania
BUL	Bulgaria	NEP	Nepal
BUR	Burkina Faso	NGR	Nigeria
CAF	Central Africa	NGU	Papua N. Guinea
CAN	Canada	NIG	Niger
CAY	Cayman Islands	NOR	Norway
CGO	Congo	NZL	New Zealand
CHA	Chad	OMA	Oman
CHI	Chile	PAK	Pakistan
CHN	Peo. Rep. China	PAN	Panama
CIV	Ivory Coast	PAR	Paraguay
CMR	Cameroon	PER	Peru
COK	Cook Islands	PHI	Philippines
COL	Colombia	POL	Poland
CRC	Costa Rica	POR	Portugal
CUB	Cuba	PRK	North Korea
CYP	Cyprus	PUR	Puerto Rico
DEN	Denmark	QAT	Qatar
DJI	Djibouti	ROM	Romania
DOM	Dominican Rep.	RWA	Rwanda
ECU	Ecuador	SAM	Western Samoa
EGY	Egypt	SAO	American Samoa
ESA	El Salvador	SEN	Senegal
ESP	Spain	SIN	Singapore
ETH	Ethiopia	SLE	Sierra Leone
FIJ	Fiji Islands	SMR	San Marino
FIN	Finland	SOL	Solomon Islands
FRA	France	SOM	Somalia
FRG	West Germany	SRI	Sri Lanka
GAB	Gabon	SUD	Sudan
GAM	Gambia	SUI	Switzerland
GBR	Great Britain	SUR	Suriname
GDR	East Germany	SWE	Sweden
GEQ	Equat. Guinea	SWZ	Swaziland
GHA	Ghana	SYR	Syria
GRE	Greece	TAN	Tanzania
GRN	Grenada	TCH	Czechoslovakia
GUA	Guatemala	TGA	Tonga
GUI	Guinea	THA	Thailand
GUM	Guam	TOG	Togo
GUY	Guyana	TPE	Chinese Taipei
HAI	Haiti	TRI	Trinidad/Tobago
HKG	Hong Kong	TUN	Tunisia
HOL	Netherlands	TUR	Turkey
HON	Honduras	UAE	U. Arab Emirates
HUN	Hungary	UGA	Uganda
INA	Indonesia	URS	Soviet Union
IND	India	URU	Uruguay
IRL	Ireland	USA	United States
IRN	Iran	VAN	Vanuatu
IRQ	Iraq	VEN	Venezuela
ISL	Iceland	VIE	Vietnam
ISR	Israel	VIN	St. Vincent/Gren's.
ISV	U.S. Virgin Islands	YAR	Yemen Arab Rep.
ITA	Italy	YMD	Yemen Dem. Rep.
IVB	British Virgin Is.	YUG	Yugoslavia
JAM	Jamaica	ZAI	Zaire
JOR	Jordan	ZAM	Zambia
JPN	Japan	ZIM	Zimbabwe

CONVERSION TABLES

cm. ⇆		in.
2.54	1	0.394
5.08	2	0.787
7.62	3	1.181
10.16	4	1.575
12.70	5	1.969
15.24	6	2.362
17.78	7	2.756
20.32	8	3.150
22.86	9	3.543
25.40	10	3.937

m. ⇆		ft.
0.305	1	3.281
0.610	2	6.562
0.914	3	9.842
1.219	4	13.123
1.524	5	16.404
1.829	6	19.685
2.134	7	22.966
2.438	8	26.247
2.743	9	29.527
3.048	10	32.808

km. ⇆		mi.
1.609	1	0.621
3.219	2	1.243
4.828	3	1.864
6.437	4	2.485
8.047	5	3.107
9.656	6	3.728
11.265	7	4.350
12.875	8	4.971
14.484	9	5.592
16.093	10	6.214

kg. ⇆		lbs.
0.454	1	2.205
0.907	2	4.409
1.361	3	6.614
1.814	4	8.818
2.268	5	11.023
2.722	6	13.228
3.175	7	15.432
3.629	8	17.637
4.082	9	19.842
4.536	10	22.046

Use numbers 1 to 10 in center column to convert to or from the metric system.
For example: 5 cm. = 1.969 in.; 15 cm. = 3.937 in. + 1.969 in. = 5.906 in.; 100 m. = 328.08 ft.
8 in. = 20.32 cm.; 4 ft. = 1.219 m.; 150 lbs. = 45.36 kg. + 22.68 kg. = 68.04 kg.

OLYMPIC GOLD MEDALS 1896 – 1984

INCLUDES ONLY EVENTS AT SEOUL

	Archery	Athletics—Track	Athletics—Field	Basketball	Boxing	Canoe/Kayak	Cycling	Diving	Equestrian	Fencing	Field Hockey	Gymnastics	Judo	Mod. Pentathlon	Rowing	Rhyth. Gymnastics	Shooting	Soccer	Swimming	Synch. Swimming	Team Handball	Tennis	Volleyball	Water Polo	Weightlifting	Wrestling	Yachting	Total
USA	5	132	99	10	42		4	43	8			14			29		19		143	2		6	1	1	14	38	8	618
URS	1	21	33	3	13	25	6	4	6	17		61	5	5	12		10	1	10		3		6	2	33	54	3	334
ITA		9	3		13		20	3	6	30		11	1	2	6		6	1				2		5	5	1		124
GDR		20	13		3	7	3	2				5			25		2	1	27		1					2	1	112
GBR		28	7		12		1		5	1	2		1		15		3	3	11			10		4		3	3	109
HUN			8		9	4				30		10		6			5	3	10					6	2	15		108
FRA		6	3		3		19		9	26		1	2		2		5	1	1			2		1	9	3	1	94
SWE		4	7			9	3	4	17	2		2		9			3	1	6						2	18	7	94
JPN		1	3		1			1				27	11		1				13			3	2			16	1	80
FIN	1	23	12		2	2						6			3		3								2	26		80
FRG		6	9		2	5	5	3	12	5	1	1	1		7		4		3						2	2	3	71
AUS		13	3				3	2							3				35					1		1		61
GER*		1	5		2	1	2	8	1			9		1	9		1		6		1			1	4	3	1	56
ROM		2	6		1	8				1		10			7		4								2	6		47
TCH		4	4		3	4	2	1	1			11			2		2	1							3	1		39
POL		7	8		8				1	4			1				2	1					1		4	1		38
HOL		4	1		1		6		5	1	1	1			3				9							1		33
CAN		6	2		2	3		1	1						3	1	4	1	6									30
SUI							1		4			14	1		4		1									4		29
BUL			1		2	1						1			2										7	13		27
TUR																										23		23
YUG				1	3	2						5	1				1	1			3			2		4		23
CUB		2	1		12					5			1										1					22
DEN					1	3	5	1	1						2		1	2								5		21
NZL		7	1		1	4			1		1				3												3	21
BEL		2			1		5		1	3		1			1		1	1								1		16
SAF*		4	1		6														1			4						16
CHN								1		1		5					3						1		4			15
ARG		2			7								1						1								2	11
AUT			1		2			1	1	1		1					1								3			11
NOR			2		1	1	1								1		2									1	1	10
MEX		3			2			1	2										1									9
IND											8																	8
KOR	1				1								2													3		7
BRA		1	2														1										2	6
EGY																									5	1		6
EST*																									1	5		6
GRE		1					1			1		1					1									1		6
KEN		6																										6
ETH		5																										5
IRL		2	2																									4
IRN																									1	3		4
JAM		4																										4
ESP							1																				2	3
PAK											3																	3
MAR		2																										2
PRK					1												1											2
URU																		2										2
BAH																											1	1
LUX		1																										1
PER																	1											1
POR		1																										1
TRI		1																										1
TUN		1																										1
UGA		1																										1
VEN					1																							1
ZIM											1																	1
	8	333	237	14	156	80	87	66	92	129	17	196	27	25	140	1	86	18	287	2	7	22	12	19	106	261	38	2466

*Estonia and Germany no longer nations. South Africa excluded since 1964.

OLYMPIC GOLD MEDALS*
BY NATION AND EVENT • 1896-1984

1988	EVENT	1984	1980	1976	1972	1968	1964	1960	1956	1952	1948	1936	1932	1928	1924	1920	1912	1908	1904	1900	1896
	ARCHERY																				
Fri 30 AM	Individual	USA	FIN	USA	USA																
Sat 1 AF	Team																				
Fri 30 AM	Individual	KOR	URS	USA	USA																
Sat 1 AF	Team																				
	ATHLETICS-TRACK																				
Fri 23 PM	100m	USA	GBR	TRI	URS	USA	USA	FRG	USA	USA	USA	USA	USA	CAN	GBR	USA	USA	SAF	USA	USA	USA
Tue 27 LN	200m	USA	ITA	JAM	URS	USA	USA	ITA	USA	USA	USA	USA	USA	CAN	USA	USA	USA	CAN	USA	USA	
Tue 27 PM	400m	USA	URS	CUB	USA	USA	USA	USA	USA	JAM	JAM	USA	USA	USA	GBR	SAF	GBR	USA	USA	USA	
Fri 30 LN	4x100m	USA	URS	USA	USA	USA	USA	FRG	USA	USA	USA	USA	USA	USA	USA	GBR					
Fri 30 LN	4x400m	USA	URS	USA	KEN	USA	USA	USA	USA	JAM	USA	GBR	USA	USA	USA	GBR	USA	USA*			
Sun 25 PM	800m	BRA	GBR	CUB	USA	AUS	NZL	NZL	USA	USA	USA	USA	GBR	GBR	GBR	GBR	USA	USA	USA	GBR	AUS
Fri 30 PM	1500m	GBR	GBR	NZL	FIN	KEN	NZL	AUS	IRL	LUX	SWE	NZL	ITA	FIN	FIN	GBR	GBR	USA	USA	GBR	AUS
Fri 30 PM	5000m	MAR	ETH	FIN	FIN	TUN	USA	NZL	URS	TCH	BEL	FIN	FIN	FIN	FIN	FRA	FIN				
Sun 25 LN-Mon AM	10,000m	ITA	ETH	FIN	FIN	KEN	USA	URS	URS	TCH	TCH	FIN	POL	FIN	FIN	FIN	FIN				
Sat 1 LN	Marathon	POR	GDR	GDR	USA	ETH	ETH	ETH	FRA	TCH	ARG	JPN	ARG	FRA	FIN	FIN	SAF	USA	USA	FRA	GRE
Sun 25 LN	110m hurdles	USA	GDR	FRA	USA	USA	USA	USA	USA	USA	USA	USA	USA	SAF	USA	CAN	USA	USA	USA	USA	USA
Sat 24 PM	400m hurdles	USA	GDR	USA	UGA	GBR	USA	USA	USA	USA	USA	USA	IRL	GBR	USA	USA		USA	USA	USA	
Thu 29 LN	3000m steeplechase	KEN	POL	SWE	KEN	KEN	BEL	POL	GBR	USA	SWE	FIN	FIN	FIN	FIN	GBR		GBR*	USA*	CAN*/USA	
Thu 22 PM-LN	20km walk	MEX	ITA	MEX	GDR	URS	GBR	URS	URS												
Thu 29 PM	50km walk	MEX	GDR		FRG	GDR	ITA	GBR	NZL	ITA	SWE	GBR	GBR								
Sat 24 PM	100m	USA	URS	FRG	GDR	USA	USA	USA	AUS	AUS	HOL	USA	POL	USA							
Thu 29 AM	200m	USA	GDR	GDR	GDR	POL	USA	USA	AUS	AUS	HOL										
Sun 25 LN	400m	USA	GDR	POL	GDR	FRA	AUS														
Fri 30 PM	4x100m	USA	GDR	GDR	FRG	USA	POL	USA	AUS	USA	HOL	USA	USA	CAN							
Fri 30 LN	4x400m	USA	URS	GDR	GDR																
Sun 25 PM	800m	ROM	URS	URS	FRG	USA	GBR	URS						GER							
Fri 30 PM	1500m	ITA	URS	URS	URS																
Sat 24 LN	3000m	ROM																			
Thu 29 LN	10,000m																				
Thu 22 PM	Marathon	USA																			
Thu 29 PM	100m hurdles	USA	URS	GDR	GDR	AUS*	GDR*	URS*	AUS*	AUS*	HOL*	ITA*	USA*								
Tue 27 PM	400m hurdles	MAR																			
	ATHLETICS—FIELD																				
Sat 24 PM	High jump	FRG	GDR	POL	URS	USA	URS	URS	USA	USA	AUS	USA	CAN	USA	USA	USA	USA	USA	USA	USA	USA
Tue 27 PM	Pole vault	FRA	POL	POL	GDR	USA	USA	USA	USA	USA	USA	USA	USA	USA	USA	USA	USA	USA	USA	USA	USA
SUN 25 LN	Long jump	USA	GDR	USA	USA	USA	GBR	USA	USA	USA	USA	USA	USA	SWE	USA	USA	USA	USA	USA	USA	USA
Fri 23 PM	Triple jump	USA	URS	URS	URS	URS	POL	POL	BRA	BRA	SWE	JPN	JPN	JPN	AUS	FIN	SWE	GBR	USA	USA	USA
Thu 22 LN-Fri AM	Shot put	ITA	URS	GDR	POL	USA	USA	USA	USA	USA	USA	GER	USA	USA	USA	FIN	USA	USA	USA	USA	USA
Fri 30 PM	Discus	FRG	URS	USA	TCH	USA	USA	USA	USA	USA	ITA	USA	USA	USA	USA	FIN	FIN	USA	USA	HUN	USA
Sat 24 PM	Javelin	FIN	URS	HUN	FRG	URS	FIN	URS	NOR	USA	FIN	GER	FIN	SWE	FIN	FIN	SWE	SWE			
Sun 25 PM	Hammer	FIN	URS	URS	URS	HUN	URS	URS	USA	HUN	HUN	GER	IRL	IRL	USA	USA	USA	USA	USA	USA	
Tue 27 PM-Thu AM	Decathlon	GBR	GBR	USA	URS	USA	FRG	USA	USA	USA	USA	USA	USA	FIN	USA	NOR	SWE/USA				
Thu 29 PM	High jump	FRG	ITA	GDR	FRG	TCH	ROM	ROM	USA	SAF	USA	HUN	USA	CAN							
Wed 28 PM	Long jump	ROM	URS	GDR	FRG	ROM	GBR	URS	POL	NZL	HUN										
Fri 30 PM	Shot put	FRG	GDR	BUL	URS	GDR	URS	URS	URS	URS	FRA										
Wed 28 PM-LN	Discus	HOL	URS	GDR	GDR	ROM	URS	URS	TCH	URS	FRA	GER	USA	POL							
Sun 25 LN	Javelin	GBR	CUB	GDR	GDR	HUN	ROM	URS	URS	TCH	AUT	GER	USA								
Thu 22 PM-Fri LN	Heptathlon/Pentathlon	AUS	URS	GDR	GDR	FRG	USA														
	BASKETBALL																				
Thu 29 PM	Men's	USA	YUG	USA	URS	USA	USA	USA	USA	USA	USA	USA									
Wed 28 PM	Women's	USA	URS	URS																	
	BOXING																				
Fri 30 PM	48kg	USA	URS	CUB	HUN	VEN															
Sat 1 PM	51kg	USA	BUL	USA	BUL	MEX	ITA	HUN	GBR	USA	ARG	GER	HUN	HUN	USA	USA			USA		
Fri 30 PM	54kg	ITA	CUB	PRK	CUB	URS	JPN	URS	FRG	FIN	HUN	ITA	CAN	ITA	SAF	SAF		GBR	USA		
Sat 1 PM	57kg	USA	GDR	CUB	URS	MEX	URS	ITA	URS	TCH	ITA	ARG	ARG	HOL	USA	FRA		GBR	USA		
Fri 30 PM	60kg	USA	CUB	USA	POL	USA	POL	POL	GBR	ITA	SAF	HUN	SAF	ITA	DEN	USA		GBR	USA		
Sat 1 PM	63.5kg	USA	ITA	USA	USA	POL	POL	TCH	URS	USA											
Fri 30 PM	67kg	USA	CUB	GDR	CUB	GDR	POL	ITA	ROM	POL	TCH	FIN	USA	NZL	BEL	CAN			USA		
Sat 1 PM	71kg	USA	CUB	POL	FRG	URS	URS	USA	HUN	HUN											
Fri 30 PM	75kg	KOR	CUB	USA	URS	GBR	URS	USA	URS	USA	HUN	FRA	USA	ITA	GBR	GBR		GBR	USA		
Sat 1 PM	81kg	YUG	YUG	USA	YUG	URS	ITA	USA	USA	USA	SAF	FRA	SAF	ARG	GBR	USA					

*Indicates closest or actual block of NBC telecast time during which final event may be shown. See p. 112 for telecast times.

TIME BLOCKS: AM=7 AM — NOON
AF=NOON — 7 PM
PM=7:30 PM — MIDNIGHT
LN=12:30 AM — 2:30 AM

* For summary by nation and sport, see page 107
• Differed slightly from current event
☐ Men   ☐ Women   ☐ Open

EVENT FINALS*	1988	EVENT	1984	1980	1976	1972	1968	1964	1960	1956	1952	1948	1936	1932	1928	1924	1920	1912	1908	1904	1900	1896
Fri 30 PM		91kg	USA																			
Sat 1 PM		91+kg	USA	CUB	CUB	CUB	USA	USA	ITA	USA	USA	ARG	GER	ARG	ARG	NOR	GBR		GBR	USA		
		CANOE/KAYAK																				
Thu 29 PM		C-1 500m	CAN	URS	URS																	
Fri 30 PM		C-1 1000m	FRG	BUL	YUG	ROM	HUN	FRG	HUN	ROM	TCH	TCH	CAN									
Thu 29 PM		C-2 500m	YUG	HUN	URS																	
Fri 30 PM		C-2 1000m	ROM	ROM	URS	URS	ROM	URS	URS	ROM	DEN	TCH	TCH									
Thu 29 PM		K-1 500m	NZL	URS	ROM																	
Fri 30 PM		K-1 1000m	NZL	GDR	GDR	URS	HUN	SWE	DEN	SWE	SWE	SWE	AUT									
Thu 29 PM		K-2 500m	NZL	URS	GDR																	
Fri 30 PM		K-2 1000m	CAN	URS	URS	URS	URS	SWE	SWE	FRG	FIN	SWE	AUT									
Fri 30 PM		K-4 1000m	NZL	GDR	URS	URS	NOR	URS														
Thu 29 PM		K-1 500m	SWE	GDR	GDR	URS	URS	URS	URS	URS	FIN	DEN										
Thu 29 PM		K-2 500m	SWE	GDR	URS	URS	FRG	FRG	URS													
Fri 30 PM		K-4 500m	ROM																			
		CYCLING																				
Mon 26 PM		Individual road race	USA	URS	SWE	HOL	ITA	ITA	URS	ITA	BEL	FRA	FRA	ITA	DEN	FRA	SWE	SAF				GRE
Sat 17 LN-Sun AM		Road team time trial	ITA	URS	URS	URS	HOL	ITA	ITA	FRA*	BEL*	BEL*	FRA*	ITA*	DEN*	FRA*	FRA*	SWE*				
Thu 22 AM		4000m individual pursuit	USA	SUI	FRG	NOR	FRA	TCH														
Sat 24 AF		4000m team pursuit	AUS	URS	FRG	FRG	DEN	FRG	ITA	ITA	ITA	FRA	FRA	ITA	ITA	ITA	ITA		GBR*			
Tue 20 AM		1km time trial	FRG	GDR	GDR	DEN	FRA	BEL	ITA	ITA	AUS	FRA	HOL	AUS	DEN							
Sat 24 AF		50km points race	BEL																			
Sat 24 AF		1000m match sprint	USA	GDR	TCH	FRA	FRA	ITA	ITA	FRA	ITA	ITA	GER	HOL	FRA	FRA	HOL				FRA*	FRA*
Sun 25 PM		Individual road race	USA																			
Sat 24 AF		1000m match sprint																				
		DIVING																				
Mon 26 PM		Platform	USA	GDR	ITA	ITA	ITA	USA	USA	MEX	USA	USA	USA	USA	USA	USA	USA	SWE	SWE	USA*		
Mon 19 PM		Springboard	USA	URS	USA	URS	USA	USA	USA	USA	USA	USA	USA	USA	USA	USA	USA	GER	GER			
Sat 17 PM		Platform	CHN	GDR	URS	SWE	TCH	USA	FRG	USA	USA	USA	USA	USA	USA	USA	DEN	SWE				
Sat 24 PM		Springboard	CAN	URS	USA	USA	USA	FRG	FRG	USA	USA	USA	USA	USA	USA	USA						
		EQUESTRIAN																				
Mon 26 LN-Tue AM		Individual dressage	FRG	AUT	SUI	FRG	URS	SUI	URS	SWE	SWE	SUI	GER	FRA	GER	SWE	SWE	SWE				
Sat 1 PM		Ind. show jumping	USA	POL	FRG	ITA	USA	FRA	ITA	FRG	FRA	MEX	GER	JPN	TCH	SUI	ITA	FRA			BEL	
Wed 21 PM-LN		Individual three day	NZL	ITA	USA	GBR	FRA	ITA	AUS	SWE	SWE	FRA	GER	HOL	HOL	HOL	SWE	SWE				
Sat 24 LN-Sun AM		Team dressage	FRG	URS	FRG	URS	FRG	FRG		SWE	SWE	FRA	GER	FRA	GER							
Tue 27 PM-LN		Team show jumping	USA	URS	FRA	FRG	CAN	FRG	FRG	FRG	GBR	MEX	GER		ESP	SWE	SWE	SWE				
Wed 21 PM-LN		Team three day	USA	URS	USA	GBR	GBR	ITA	AUS	GBR	SWE	USA	GER	USA	HOL	HOL	SWE	SWE				
		FENCING																				
Wed 21 AM		Individual foil	ITA	URS	ITA	POL	ROM	POL	URS	FRA	FRA	FRA	ITA	ITA	FRA	FRA	ITA	ITA		CUB	FRA	FRA
Sat 24 AF		Individual epee	FRA	SWE	FRG	HUN	HUN	URS	ITA	ITA	ITA	ITA	ITA	ITA	FRA	BEL	FRA	BEL	FRA	CUB	CUB	
Fri 23 AM		Individual saber	FRA	URS	URS	URS	POL	HUN	HUN	HUN	HUN	HUN	HUN	HUN	HUN	HUN	ITA	HUN	HUN	CUB	FRA	GRE
Tue 27 AM		Team foil	ITA	FRA	FRG	POL	FRA	URS	URS	ITA	FRA	FRA	ITA	FRA	ITA	ITA				CUB		
Fri 30 AM		Team epee	FRG	FRA	SWE	HUN	HUN	HUN	ITA	ITA	ITA	FRA	ITA	FRA	ITA	FRA	ITA	BEL	FRA			
Thu 29 AM		Team saber	ITA	URS	URS	ITA	URS	URS	HUN	HUN	HUN	HUN	HUN	HUN	HUN	ITA	ITA	HUN	HUN			
Thu 22 AM		Individual foil	CHN	FRA	HUN	ITA	URS	HUN	FRG	GBR	ITA	HUN	HUN	AUT	GER	DEN						
Wed 28 AM		Team foil	FRG	FRA	URS	URS	URS	HUN	URS													
		FIELD HOCKEY																				
Fri 30 LN-Sat AF		Men's	PAK	IND	NZL	FRG	PAK	IND	PAK	IND	IND	IND	IND	IND	IND		GBR		GBR			
Thu 29 LN-Fri AM		Women's	HOL	ZIM																		
		GYMNASTICS																				
Fri 23 PM-LN		Floor exercise	CHN	GDR	URS	URS	JPN	ITA	JPN	URS	SWE	HUN	SUI	HUN								
Fri 23 PM-LN		Horizontal bar	JPN	BUL	JPN	JPN	JPN/URS	URS	JPN	JPN	SUI	SUI	FIN	USA	SUI	YUG				USA		GER
Fri 23 PM-LN		Pommel horse	CHN/USA	HUN	HUN	URS	YUG	YUG	URS/FIN	URS	URS	FIN	GER	HUN	SUI	SUI				USA		SUI
Fri 23 PM-LN		Vault	CHN	URS	URS	GDR	URS	JPN	URS/JPN	URS/FRG	URS	FIN	GER	ITA	SUI	USA				USA		GER
Fri 23 PM-LN		Parallel bars	USA	URS	JPN	JPN	JPN	JPN	URS	URS	SUI	SUI	GER	ITA	TCH	SUI				USA		GER
Fri 23 PM-LN		Rings	CHN/JPN	URS	URS	JPN	JPN	JPN	URS	URS	URS	SUI	TCH	USA	USA	ITA				USA		GRE
Wed 21 PM-LN		All-around	JPN	URS	URS	JPN	JPN	JPN	URS	URS	URS	FIN	GER	ITA*	SUI*	YUG*	ITA*	ITA*	ITA*	AUT*	FRA*	
Tue 20 AM		Team competition	USA	URS	JPN	JPN	JPN	JPN	JPN	URS	URS	FIN	GER	ITA*	SUI*	ITA*		SWE*		USA*		
Sat 24 PM-LN		Floor exercise	ROM	URS/ROM	URS	URS	TCH/URS	URS	URS	URS/HUN	HUN											
Sat 24 PM-LN		Uneven parallel bars	USA/CHN	GDR	ROM	GDR	TCH	URS	URS	HUN	HUN											
Sat 24 PM-LN		Balance beam	ROM/ROM	ROM	ROM	URS	URS	TCH	TCH	HUN	URS											
Sat 24 PM-LN		Vault	ROM	URS	URS	GDR	TCH	TCH	URS	URS	URS											
Thu 22 PM		All-around	USA	URS	ROM	URS	TCH	TCH	URS	URS	URS											
Wed 21 AM		Team competition	ROM	URS	URS	URS	URS	URS	URS	URS*	URS*	TCH*	GER*		HOL*							
		JUDO																				
Sun 25 AM		60kg	JPN	FRA	CUB*	JPN*		JPN*														
Mon 26 AM		65kg	JPN	URS																		
Tue 27 AM		71kg	KOR	ITA	URS*	JPN*																

*See bottom of page 108.

EVENT FINALS*	1988	EVENT	1984	1980	1976	1972	1968	1964	1960	1956	1952	1948	1936	1932	1928	1924	1920	1912	1908	1904	1900	1896
Wed 28 AM		78kg	FRG	URS	JPN*	JPN*		JPN*														
Thu 29 AM		86kg	AUT	SUI																		
Fri 30 AM		95kg	KOR	BEL	JPN*	URS*																
Sat 1 AF		95+kg	JPN	FRA	URS	HOL		JPN														
		MODERN PENTATHLON																				
Wed 21 PM		Individual	ITA	URS	POL	HUN	SWE	HUN	HUN	SWE	SWE	SWE	GER	SWE	SWE	SWE	SWE	SWE				
Wed 21 PM		Team	ITA	URS	GBR	URS	HUN	URS	HUN	URS	HUN											
		RHYTHMIC GYMNASTICS																				
Fri 30 AM		All-around	CAN																			
		ROWING																				
Fri 23 PM		Single scull	FIN	FIN	FIN	URS	HOL	URS	URS	URS	URS	AUS	GER	AUS	AUS	GBR	USA	GBR	GBR	USA	FRA	
Fri 23 PM		Double scull	USA	GDR	NOR	URS	URS	URS	TCH	URS	ARG	GBR	GBR	USA	USA	USA	USA			USA		
Sat 24 PM		Quadruple scull	FRG	GDR	GDR																	
Fri 23 PM		Coxless pair	ROM	GDR	GDR	GDR	GDR	CAN	URS	USA	USA	GBR	GER	GBR	GER	HOL			GBR	USA*		
Sat 24 PM		Coxless four	NZL	GDR	GDR	GDR	GDR	DEN	USA	CAN	YUG	ITA	GER	GBR	GBR	GBR			GBR	USA		
Sat 24 PM		Coxed pair	ITA	GDR	GDR	GDR	ITA	USA	FRG	USA	FRA	DEN	GER	USA	SUI	SUI	ITA				HOL	
Fri 23 PM		Coxed four	GBR	GDR	URS	FRG	NZL	FRG	FRG	ITA	TCH	USA	GER	GER	ITA	SUI	SUI	GER			GER	
Sat 24 PM		Coxed eight	CAN	GDR	GDR	NZL	FRG	USA	FRG	USA	USA	USA	GER	GER	USA	USA	USA	GBR	GBR	USA	USA	
Fri 23 PM		Single scull	ROM	ROM	GDR																	
Fri 23 PM		Double scull	ROM	URS	BUL																	
Sat 24 PM		Quadruple scull	ROM	GDR	GDR																	
Fri 23 PM		Coxless pair	ROM	GDR	BUL																	
Fri 23 PM		Coxed four	ROM	GDR	GDR																	
Sat 24 PM		Coxed eight	USA	GDR	GDR																	
		SHOOTING																				
Thu 22 AM		Free rifle	GBR	HUN	FRG	PRK	TCH	HUN	FRG	CAN	ROM	USA	NOR	SWE		FRA	USA	USA	GBR			
Tue 20 AM		Air rifle	FRA																			
Mon 19 AM		English match rifle	USA	URS	USA	USA	FRG	USA	URS	URS	NOR											
Sun 18 AM		Free pistol	CHN	URS	GDR	SWE	URS	FIN	URS	FIN	USA	PER	SWE			USA	USA				SUI	USA
Fri 23 AM		Rapid-fire pistol	JPN	ROM	GDR	POL	POL	FIN	USA	ROM	HUN	HUN	GER	ITA		USA	BRA	USA	BEL		FRA	GRE
Fri 23 AM		Running game target	CHN	URS	URS	URS															FRA	
Sat 24 AF		Air pistol																				
Wed 21 AM		Standard rifle	CHN																			
Sun 18 AM		Air rifle	USA																			
Mon 19 AM		Sport pistol	CAN																			
Wed 21 AM		Air pistol																				
Sat 24 AF		Skeet	USA	DEN	TCH	FRG	URS															
Tue 20 AM		Trap	ITA	ITA	USA	ITA	GBR	ITA	ROM	ITA	CAN				HUN	USA	USA	CAN			FRA	
		SOCCER																				
Sat 1 AF		Men's	FRA	TCH	GDR	POL	HUN	HUN	YUG	URS	HUN	SWE	ITA		URU	URU	BEL	GBR	GBR	CAN	GBR	
		SWIMMING																				
Sat 24 AF		50m freestyle																		HUN		
Thu 22 AM		100m freestyle	USA	GDR	USA	USA	AUS	USA	AUS	AUS	USA	USA	HUN	JPN	USA	USA	USA	USA	USA	HUN*		HUN
Sun 18 PM		200m freestyle	FRG	URS	USA	USA	AUS													USA*		AUS
Fri 23 AM		400m freestyle	USA	URS	USA	AUS	USA	USA	AUS	AUS	FRA	USA	USA	USA	ARG	USA	USA	CAN	GBR	USA*		AUT
Sun 25 AM		1500m freestyle	USA	URS	USA	USA	USA	AUS	AUS	AUS	USA	USA	JPN	JPN	SWE	AUS	USA	CAN	GBR	GER*	GBR*	HUN*
Sun 18 PM		100m breaststroke	USA	GBR	USA	JPN	USA															
Fri 23 AM		200m breaststroke	CAN	URS	GBR	USA	MEX	AUS	USA	JPN	AUS	USA	JPN	JPN	JPN	USA	SWE	GER	GBR			
Tue 20 PM		100m butterfly	FRG	SWE	USA	USA	USA															
Sat 24 AF		200m butterfly	AUS	URS	USA	USA	USA	AUS	USA	USA												
Sat 24 AF		100m backstroke	USA	SWE	USA	GDR	GDR		AUS	AUS	USA	USA	USA	JPN	USA	USA	USA	USA	GER	GER*		
Thu 22 AM		200m backstroke	USA	HUN	USA	GDR	GDR	USA													GER	
Sun 25 AM		200m ind. medley	CAN			SWE	USA															
Tue 20 PM		400m ind. medley	CAN	URS	USA	SWE	USA	USA														
Fri 23 AM		4x100m freestyle relay	USA			USA	USA	USA														
Tue 20 PM		4x200m freestyle relay	USA	URS	USA	USA	USA	USA	USA	AUS	USA	USA	JPN	JPN	USA	USA	USA	AUS	GBR			
Sun 25 AM		4x100m medley relay	USA	AUS	USA	USA	USA	USA	USA													
Sun 25 AM		50m freestyle																				
Sun 18 PM		100m freestyle	USA USA	GDR	GDR	USA	USA	AUS	AUS	AUS	HUN	DEN	HOL	USA	USA	USA	USA	AUS				
Tue 20 PM		200m freestyle	USA	GDR	GDR	AUS	USA															
Thu 22 AM		400m freestyle	USA	GDR	GDR	AUS	USA	USA	USA	AUS	HUN	USA	HOL	USA	USA	USA	USA*					
Sat 24 AF		800m freestyle	USA	AUS	GDR	USA	USA															
Fri 23 AM		100m breaststroke	HOL	GDR	GDR	USA	YUG															
Tue 20 PM		200m breaststroke	CAN	URS	URS	AUS	USA	URS	GBR	FRG	HUN	HOL	JPN	AUS	GER	GBR						
Fri 23 AM		100m butterfly	USA	GDR	GDR	JPN	AUS	USA	USA	USA												
Sun 25 AM		200m butterfly	USA	GDR	GDR	USA	HOL															
Thu 22 AM		100m backstroke	USA	GDR	GDR	USA	USA	USA	USA	GBR	SAF	DEN	HOL	USA	HOL	USA						
Sun 25 AM		200m backstroke	HOL	GDR	GDR	USA	USA															

*See bottom of page 108.

EVENT FINALS*	1988	EVENT	1984	1980	1976	1972	1968	1964	1960	1956	1952	1948	1936	1932	1928	1924	1920	1912	1908	1904	1900	1896
Sat 24 AF		200m ind. medley	USA			AUS	USA																
Sun 18 PM		400m ind. medley	USA	GDR	GDR	AUS	USA	USA															
Thu 22 AM		4x100m freestyle relay	USA	GDR	USA	USA	USA	USA	USA	AUS	HUN	USA	HOL	USA	USA	USA	USA	GBR				
Sat 24 AF		4x100m medley relay	USA	GDR	GDR	USA	USA	USA	USA													
		SYNCHRONIZED SWIMMING																					
Thu 29 PM		Solo	USA																				
Fri 30 PM		Duet	USA																				
		TABLE TENNIS																					
Sat 1 AF		Singles																					
Fri 30 AM		Doubles																					
Sat 1 AF		Singles																					
Fri 30 AM		Doubles																					
		TEAM HANDBALL																					
Sat 1 AF		Men's	YUG	GDR	URS	YUG																	
Mon 26 LN-Thu AM		Women's	YUG	URS	URS																		
		TENNIS																					
Thu 29 PM-LN		Singles														USA	SAF	SAF	GBR	USA	GBR		GBR
Fri 30 PM-LN		Doubles														USA	GBR	SAF	GBR	USA	GBR		GBR GER
Fri 30 PM-LN		Singles														USA	FRA	FRA	GBR		GBR		
Thu 29 PM-LN		Doubles														USA	GBR						
		VOLLEYBALL																					
Sat 1 PM		Men's	USA	URS	POL	JPN	URS	URS															
Thu 29 AM		Women's	CHN	URS	JPN	URS	URS	JPN															
		WATER POLO																					
Sat 1 AF		Men's	YUG	URS	HUN	URS	YUG	HUN	ITA	HUN	HUN	ITA	HUN	HUN	GER	FRA	GBR	GBR	GBR	USA	GBR		
		WEIGHTLIFTING																					
Sun 18 AM		52kg	CHN	URS	URS	POL																	
Mon 19 AM		56kg	CHN	CUB	BUL	HUN	IRN	URS	USA	USA	URS	USA											
Tue 20 AM		60kg	CHN	URS	URS	BUL	JPN	JPN	URS	USA	URS	EGY	USA	FRA	AUT	ITA*	BEL*						
Wed 21 AM		67.5kg	CHN	BUL	URS	URS	POL	POL	URS	URS	USA	EGY	AUT EGY	FRA	AUT GER	FRA*	EST*						
Thu 22 AM		75kg	FRG	BUL	BUL	BUL	URS	TCH	URS	URS	USA	USA	EGY	GER	FRA	ITA*	FRA*						
Sat 24 AF		82.5kg	ROM	URS	URS	NOR	URS	URS	POL	USA	URS	USA	FRA	FRA	EGY	FRA*	FRA*						
Sun 25 AM		90kg	ROM	HUN	URS	BUL	FIN	URS	URS	URS	USA												
Mon 26 AM		100kg	FRG	TCH																			
Tue 27 AM		110kg	ITA	URS	URS	URS	URS	URS	URS	USA	USA	USA	GER	TCH	GER	ITA*	ITA*						
Wed 28 PM		110+kg	AUS	URS	URS	URS																	
		WRESTLING																					
Thu 29 AM		48kg freestyle	USA	ITA	BUL	URS														USA			
Fri 30 AM		52kg freestyle	YUG	URS	JPN	JPN	JPN	IRN	TUR	URS	TUR	FIN								USA			
Sat 1 AF		57kg freestyle	JPN	URS*	URS	JPN	JPN	JPN	USA	TUR	JPN	TUR	HUN*	USA*	FIN*	FIN*				USA	USA		
Thu 29 AM		62kg freestyle	USA	URS	KOR	URS	JPN*	JPN*	TUR	JPN	TUR	TUR	FIN*	FIN*	USA*	USA*	USA*			GBR*	USA*		
Sat 1 AF		68kg freestyle	KOR	URS	URS	USA	IRN*	BUL*	USA*	IRN*	SWE*	TUR*	HUN*	FRA*	EST*	USA*	FIN*				USA*		
Fri 30 AM		74kg freestyle	USA	BUL	JPN	USA	TUR*	TUR*	USA*	JPN*	USA*	TUR*	USA*	USA*	FIN*	SUI*					USA*		
Sat 1 AF		82kg freestyle	USA	BUL	USA	URS	URS*	BUL*	TUR*	BUL*	URS*	USA*	FRA*	SWE*	SUI*	SUI*	FIN*			GBR*			
Thu 29 AM		90kg freestyle	USA	URS	URS	USA	TUR*	URS*	TUR*	IRN*	SWE*	USA*	SWE*	USA*	SWE*	USA*	SWE*						
Fri 30 AM		100kg freestyle	USA	URS	URS	URS																	
Sat 1 AF		100-130kg freestyle	USA	URS	URS	URS*	URS*	URS*	FRG*	TUR*	URS*	HUN*	EST*	SWE*	SWE*	USA*	SUI*			GBR*	USA*		
Tue 20 AM		48kg Greco-Roman	ITA	URS	URS	ROM																	
Wed 21 AM		52kg Greco-Roman	JPN	URS	URS	BUL	BUL	JPN	ROM	URS	URS	ITA											
Thu 22 AM		57kg Greco-Roman	FRG	URS	FIN	URS	HUN	JPN	URS	URS	HUN	SWE	HUN*	GER*	GER*	EST*							
Tue 20 AM		62kg Greco-Roman	KOR	GRE	POL	BUL	URS*	HUN*	TUR	FIN	TUR	TUR	TUR*	ITA*	EST*	FIN*	FIN*	FIN*					
Thu 22 AM		68kg Greco-Roman	YUG	ROM	URS	URS	JPN*	TUR*	TUR*	FIN*	URS*	SWE*	FIN*	SWE*	HUN*	FIN*	FIN*	FIN*	ITA*				
Wed 21 AM		74kg Greco-Roman	FIN	HUN	URS	TCH	GDR*	URS*	TUR*	TUR*	HUN*	SWE*	SWE*	SWE*									
Thu 22 AM		82kg Greco-Roman	ROM	URS	YUG	HUN	GDR*	YUG*	BUL*	URS*	SWE*	SWE*	SWE*	FIN*	FIN*	FIN*	SWE*	SWE*	SWE*				
Tue 20 AM		90kg Greco-Roman	USA	HUN	URS	URS	BUL*	BUL*	TUR*	URS*	FIN*	SWE*	SWE*	EGY*	SWE*	SWE*			FIN*				
Wed 21 AM		100kg Greco-Roman	ROM	BUL	URS	ROM																	
Thu 22 AM		100-130kg Greco-Roman	USA	URS	URS	URS	HUN*	HUN*	URS*	URS*	URS*	TUR*	EST*	SWE*	SWE*	FRA*	FIN*	FIN*	HUN*				GER*
		YACHTING																					
Mon 26 AM		Star	USA	URS		AUS	USA	BAH	URS	USA	ITA	USA	GER	USA									
Mon 26 AM		Finn	NZL	FIN	GDR	FRA	URS	FRG	DEN	DEN	DEN												
Mon 26 AM		Flying Dutchman	USA	ESP	FRG	GBR	GBR	NZL	NOR														
Mon 26 AM		Soling	USA	DEN	DEN	USA																	
Mon 26 AM		Tornado	NZL	BRA	GBR																		
Mon 26 AM		Windglider	HOL																				
Mon 26 AM		470	ESP	BRA	FRG																		
Mon 26 AM		470																					

*See bottom of page 108.

• Differed slightly from current event.

☐ Men   ☐ Women   ☐ Open

NBC TELECAST TIMES* • SPORTS SCHEDULE

FOR SCHEDULE OF EVENT FINALS SEE PAGES 108-111, COLUMN ONE.

EASTERN DAYLIGHT TIME

SEPT/OCT 1988

	16 FRI	17 SAT	18 SUN	19 MON	20 TUE	21 WED	22 THU	23 FRI	24 SAT	25 SUN	26 MON	27 TUE	28 WED	29 THU	30 FRI	1 SAT	2 SUN
Time slots	8 PM-MIDN'T	4-7 PM / 7:30 PM-2:30 AM*	8 AM-NOON / 4-7 PM / 7:30 PM-2:30 AM*		7 AM-10 AM / 4 PM-5 PM / 7:30 PM-2:30 AM*				NOON-1 PM / 4-7 PM / 7:30 PM-2:30 AM*	8 AM-NOON / 4-7 PM / 7:30 PM-2:30 AM*		7 AM-10 AM / 4 PM-5 PM / 7:30 PM-2:30 AM*				NOON-1 PM / 4-7 PM / 7:30 PM-2:30 AM*	8 AM-NOON / 7 PM-11 PM
ARCHERY																	
ATHLETICS-TRACK																	
ATHLETICS-FIELD																	
BASKETBALL																	
BOXING																	
CANOE/KAYAK																	
CYCLING																	
DIVING																	
EQUESTRIAN																	
FENCING																	
FIELD HOCKEY																	
GYMNASTICS																	
JUDO																	
MODERN PENTATHLON																	
RHYTHMIC GYMNASTICS																	
ROWING																	
SHOOTING																	
SOCCER																	
SWIMMING																	
SYNCH. SWIMMING																	
TABLE TENNIS																	
TEAM HANDBALL																	
TENNIS																	
VOLLEYBALL																	
WATER POLO																	
WEIGHTLIFTING																	
WRESTLING																	
YACHTING																	
CEREMONIES	Opening																Closing

* NBC telecast times as of 6/1/88.
* Local programming Midnight to 12:30 AM

Legend: ▓ Men ▒ Women ☐ Open